ECO DESIGN

FURNITURE
MEUBLES
MUEBLES
MOBILIÁRIO

promopress

ECO DESIGN
Furniture / Meubles / Muebles / Mobiliário

Copyright © 2013 DOPRESS BOOKS
Copyright © 2013 English, French, Spanish and Portuguese edition
published by Promopress for sale worldwide except China.

Translation: English (revision) / French / Spanish / Brazilian Portuguese:
Tom Corkett / Marie-Pierre Teuler / Juan José Llanos Collado / Élcio Carillo
Layout & cover design: Gemma Alberich

PROMOPRESS is a brand of:
Promotora de Prensa Internacional S.A.
C/ Ausiàs March 124
08013 Barcelona, Spain
Phone: +34 93 245 14 64
Fax: +34 93 265 48 83
info@promopress.es
www.promopress.es
www.promopresseditions.com
Facebook & Twitter: Promopress Editions @PromopressEd

Edited by Dopress

ISBN: 978-84-92810-84-0

Printed in China.

ECO DESIGN

FURNITURE
MEUBLES
MUEBLES
MOBILIÁRIO

ESP

Eco Design: Muebles, tiene como objetivo presentar los muebles ecológicos más actuales de los principales equipos de diseño del mundo; asimismo, anima a las personas, y especialmente a los diseñadores profesionales, a adoptar una postura más responsable con el medio ambiente en sus ideas y procesos de diseño. Centrado en las aplicaciones de los conceptos del eco-diseño, las ideas respetuosas con el medio ambiente y las tecnologías para el ahorro de energía, este conjunto de libros tiene como objetivo convertirse en una excelente fuente de inspiración para diseñadores y artistas.

POR

Desing Eco: Mobiliário tem por objetivo apresentar as peças mais atuais de móveis eco das principais equipes de design do mundo; ao mesmo tempo, animar as pessoas, e especialmente os Designers profissionais, a conferir às suas ideias e processos de design um enfoque mais consciente a nível ambiental. Centrado nas aplicações de conceitos de eco design, ideias a favor do meio ambiente e tecnologias de economia de energia, este conjunto de livros tem por objetivo constituir uma excelente fonte de inspiração para designers e artistas.

FRA

Eco Design: Meubles, s'attache à présenter les toutes dernières créations des meilleurs designers de meubles de la planète. Il a aussi pour but d'encourager les gens, en particulier les professionnels du design, à adopter une démarche tenant compte de l'environnement lors de la mise au point de concepts et de procédés de fabrication. Les deux volumes se concentrent sur les applications du design écologique, les idées respectueuses de l'environnement et les technologies d'économie d'énergie. Ils seront une grande source d'inspiration pour les designers et les artistes attirés par l'éco-design.

ECO DESIGN: FURNITURE, AIMS TO PRESENT THE LATEST ECO-FURNITURE PIECES FROM THE WORLD'S LEADING DESIGN TEAMS, AS WELL AS ENCOURAGE MORE PEOPLE, AND ESPECIALLY PROFESSIONAL DESIGNERS, TO CONSIDER A MORE ENVIRONMENTALLY CONSCIOUS APPROACH TO THEIR DESIGN IDEAS AND PROCESSES. FOCUSING ON THE APPLICATIONS OF ECO-DESIGN CONCEPTS, ENVIRONMENTALLY FRIENDLY IDEAS, AND ENERGY-SAVING TECHNOLOGIES, THIS SET OF BOOKS AIMS TO BE AN EXCELLENT AND INSPIRING RESOURCE FOR DESIGNERS AND ARTISTS.

01/ 08
RECYCLING & REUSE

RECYCLAGE ET RÉEMPLOI
RECICLAJE Y REUTILIZACIÓN
RECICLAGEM E REUTILIZAÇÃO

02/ 56
NATURAL MATERIALS

MATÉRIAUX NATURELS
MATERIALES NATURALES
MATERIAIS NATURAIS

5¢ **10**
FF1 Felt Chair **12**
NOBODY & Little **14**
NOBODY Chairs
SPOOK **15**
Rubber Stool **16**
Transit Chairs & Tables **17**
Recycled Foam Soft Pad
Couch and Armchair **18**
Latex Roll **19**
Pouf de Paille **20**
Incasso Durable Furniture **21**
Annie the Shopping
Trolley Chair **22**
Max the Bath Tub Chaise **22**
Silvana the Wash
Drum Table **23**
Back in the Saddle **23**
Puffy, Tied & Tired **24**
Spring Bed **25**
RE: cover **26**
Rip + Tatter Kid's Chair **27**
Three Little Pigs **28**

Papton **30**
Piao-Paper Chair **31**
Chair 4A **32**
The Rubens Collection **34**
CAST Collection **36**
Sketch Collection **38**
Hockenheimer **40**
Endless **41**
Processed Paper **42**
Paperpulp **44**
DVELAS **46**
Not So Fragile **48**
RD Legs Chair **50**
Pandora **51**
Stump Series **52**
Blockshelf **53**
The Patchwork
Collection **54**

Upside Down Lounge **58**
Tamed Nature Stool **59**
Magistral Cabinet **60**
Bamboo Cell No.2 **62**
Bamboo Cell **63**
Barca **64**
Fjarill **65**
Baum **66**
Endless Table **67**
Clamp Chair **68**
Schmöbel Shoe Cabinet **69**
VIKA Coffee Table **69**
Atlas Chair **70**
Staircase **72**
3×3 **73**
Flezi **74**
Sheep Chair **75**
HUSH **76**
Livingstones **78**
Le Hasard **79**
16/45 End Table **80**
Cyclone Lounger **81**
Marbelous **82**

Zeed **84**
3 Blocks **85**
Wooden Hammock **86**
Alvisilkchair **87**
Loopita **88**
Chaise Longue No.4 **89**
Kaguya-Hime **90**
E.I.S **91**
Vita, Equus and Servus **92**
Get Up Esparto Grass **94**
Eyrie Chair **95**
Nest **96**
Elda Chair **97**
Ziggy and Zaggy **98**
De Tafelwip /
The Curtessy Table **99**
Stump and Trunk **100**
Shavings **101**

03/ 102
TECHNOLOGY & CRAFTS

TECHNOLOGIE ET ARTISANAT
TECNOLOGÍA Y ARTESANÍA
TECNOLOGIA E ARTES

04/ 142
OTHER ECO APPROACHES

AUTRES APPROCHES ÉCOLOGIQUES
OTRAS TENDENCIAS ECOLÓGICAS
OUTROS ENFOQUES ECO

Cabbage Chair **104**
Transparent Chair **105**
EVA Chair for Kids **106**
Ivy Chair **107**
Hut-Hut **108**
PANE Chair **110**
Flux Chair **112**
Stitching Concrete **114**
Poured Wood **115**
The Coiling Collection **116**
Tailored Stool **117**
Gaudi Chair **118**
C Bench **120**
Plum Stool **121**
Drombo **122**
TRON Armchair **123**
Munken Cube **124**
TOPO Tables **125**
Softseating Fanning Stool **126**
Flood Stool **128**
The Inner Life **129**
Peacock Chair **130**
Pressed Chair **131**

UnPølished **132**
Trash Cube **133**
Dune **134**
Alien **136**
Tufty **137**
Magic Magnus Mountain **138**
Succession **140**

Spinning Chair Accelerator **144**
Darwin Chair **146**
Plantable **147**
HOX – Soft and Folding Furniture **148**
Montanara **150**
Piccola Via Lattea **151**
The Idea of a Tree **152**
Parasite Farm **154**

INDEX

01

08-55

FRA

RECYCLAGE ET RÉEMPLOI

Parmi les produits recyclés entrant dans la fabrication des meubles présentés dans cet ouvrage, on retrouve le verre, le papier, le métal, le plastique, les textiles, les matières organiques et de nombreux autres matériaux écologiques. Tous ont été utilisés de manière créative pour produire des meubles branchés et originaux.

ESP

RECICLAJE Y REUTILIZACIÓN

Todos los materiales reciclados empleados en los muebles que les presentamos en este libro, que incluyen vidrio, papel, metal, plástico, tejidos y materiales orgánicos, sin olvidar otros materiales respetuosos con el medioambiente, se han usado de manera creativa para producir unos muebles realmente sensacionales y únicos.

POR

RECICLAGEM E REUTILIZAÇÃO

Os materiais reciclados usados nos móveis que lhes apresentamos neste livro, que incluem vidro, papel, metal, plástico, tecido e materiais orgânicos, sem esquecer, além disso, outros materiais favoráveis ao meio ambiente, foram todos usados de forma criativa para produzir móveis autenticamente sensacionais e únicos.

RECYCLING & REUSE

The recycled materials used in the furniture featured in this book, which include glass, paper, metal, plastic, textiles, and organic materials, not to mention other environmentally friendly materials besides, have all been used creatively to produce some truly cool and unique pieces of furniture.

5¢ (5 CENTS)

DESIGN FIRM
Mark Reigelman

DESIGNER
Mark A. Reigelman II

PHOTOGRAPHY
Norman Nelson & Jared Zagha

CLIENT
Heller Gallery

The 5 Cents collection is inspired by the protective glass barriers, found on fences and rooftops, that surround homes all over the world. Twelve typical household objects, including books, chairs, lights, and bear skin rugs, have been encrusted with protective layers of broken glass. These objects were selected based on their symbolic and utilitarian importance within the home. By fusing elements of protection with objects found within the home, the 5 Cents collection debates the need for fervent homestead defense while pointing out the repercussions of overprotection and the impact it has on social dialogue. The 5 Cents collection uses over a thousand pounds of 100 percent recycled glass and twenty gallons of epoxy. The glass is broken, tumbled, and then attached to an armature. Layer by layer the objects slowly grow until each is encrusted with over forty layers of glass shards.

FRA
La collection 5 Cents s'inspire des tessons de verre que l'on place au sommet des murs d'une propriété pour en protéger l'accès, et que l'on retrouve partout dans le monde. Douze objets domestiques courants, dont des livres, des chaises, des lampes et des tapis ont été incrustés de plusieurs couches protectrices de verre brisé. Ces articles ont été choisis pour la place symbolique et utilitaire qu'ils tiennent dans la maison. En bardant des objets domestiques de matériel de protection, le designer a voulu montrer le danger que représente la défense excessive des biens et son impact sur le dialogue social. La collection 5 Cents fait appel à plus de 450 kilos de verre 100 % recyclé et 75 litres d'époxy. Le verre est cassé et broyé puis fixé à une armature. Couche après couche, les objets prennent peu à peu leur forme jusqu'à ce qu'ils soient enveloppés de quarante épaisseurs de particules de verre.

ESP
La colección 5 Cents se inspira en las barreras protectoras de cristales que se encuentran en las tapias y los tejados de las casas de todo el mundo. Se han incrustado capas protectoras de cristales rotos en doce objetos domésticos típicos, como libros, sillas, lámparas y alfombras de piel de oso. Estos objetos fueron seleccionados en función de su importancia simbólica y utilitaria en el hogar. Al fusionar elementos de protección con objetos que se encuentran dentro del hogar, la colección 5 Cents cuestiona la necesidad de una acérrima defensa de la casa, al tiempo que sugiere las repercusiones de la sobreprotección y el impacto que esta tiene sobre el diálogo social. La colección 5 Cents emplea más de 450 kilos de vidrio 100 % reciclado, así como 75 litros de resina epoxi. El vidrio se rompe, se tira y seguidamente se adhiere a un armazón. Los objetos crecen poco a poco, una capa tras otra, hasta que quedan cubiertos con más de cuarenta capas de esquirlas.

POR
A coleção 5 Cents inspira-se nas barreiras protetoras de vidro, encontradas nas cercas e telhados ao redor de casas em todo o mundo. Incrustaram-se camadas protetoras de vidro picado em doze objetos típicos domésticos, incluídos livros, cadeiras, luzes e tapetes de pele de urso. Estes objetos foram selecionados com base em sua importância simbólica e utilitária dentro do lar. Ao fundir elementos de proteção com objetos que se encontram dentro do lar, a coleção 5 Cents discute a necessidade de uma fervorosa defesa da propriedade, ao mesmo tempo que aponta as repercussões da superproteção e o impacto que tem sobre o diálogo social. A coleção 5 Cents usa mais de 1.000 libras de vidro 100 % reciclado e 20 galões de resina epóxi. O vidro se quebra, se revira e depois se junta a uma armação. Camada após camada, os objetos crescem lentamente até que cada um fica incrustado com mais de quarenta camadas de vidro picado.

FF1 FELT CHAIR

DESIGN FIRM
Fox & Freeze

PHOTOGRAPHY
Tom De Vrieze

DESIGNER
James Van Vossel & Tom De Vrieze

CLIENT
Fox & Freeze

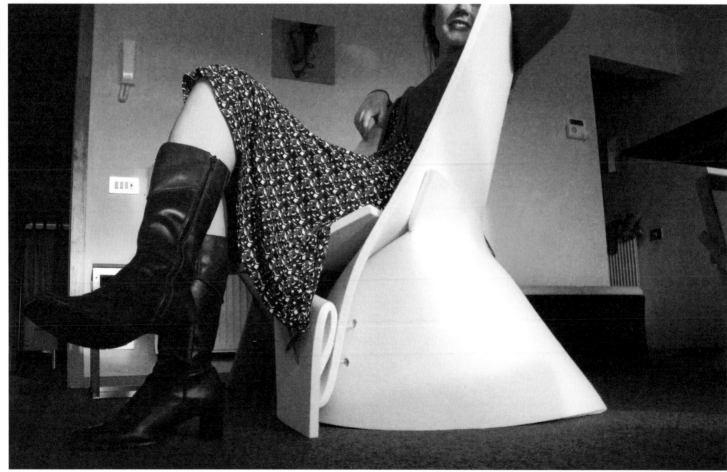

The FF1 Felt Chair is an indoor lounge chair made out of a single square sheet of synthetic felt. There is no loss of material other than from the drilled holes. The chair does not have a frame made from wood, metal, or any other material, and instead has a self-supporting structure. The flax rope contracts the chair and finishes it off aesthetically. The shell and base are not made separately from the sheet, and instead both remain part of the original square surface. The felt sheet is twisted and twisted again, just like a scarf, ultimately creating an object that is both symmetrical and yet also asymmetrical. With this chair, form literally follows function.

FRA

Le FF1 est un fauteuil d'intérieur fabriqué dans une seule plaque carrée en feutre synthétique. Il n'y a aucune perte de matière, sauf à l'endroit des perforations. La structure du fauteuil n'est ni en bois ni en métal ni en aucun autre matériau similaire : elle n'en a pas besoin car elle est autoporteuse. La corde en lin a une fonction de contraction et ajoute une touche esthétique. La coquille et la base du fauteuil ne sont pas des éléments sèparés, mais font partie intégrante de la plaque en feutre. Celle-ci est pliée plusieurs fois à la manière d'un foulard, de manière à former un objet à la fois symétrique et asymétrique. Ce fauteuil illustre parfaitement le principe suivant lequel la forme suit la fonction.

ESP

La silla de fieltro FF1 es una silla de salón, fabricada con un trecho cuadrado de fieltro sintético. Se aprovechan todos los materiales excepto el de los agujeros perforados. La silla no tiene un armazón de madera, de metal ni de otros materiales, sino que cuenta con una estructura que se sustenta sola. La cuerda de lino sujeta la silla y le da un acabado estético. La carcasa y la base no están separadas de la lámina de fieltro; antes al contrario, ambas forman parte de la superficie cuadrada original. El retal se dobla y se vuelve a doblar, a la manera de una bufanda, resultando en un objeto que es al mismo tiempo simétrico y asimétrico. Con esta silla, la forma sigue literalmente a la función.

POR

A cadeira de feltro FF1 é uma cadeira de salão para interiores, fabricada com uma única lâmina quadrada de feltro sintético. Não há nenhuma outra perda de material além dos furos realizados. A cadeira não tem uma estrutura de madeira, metal ou qualquer outro material, mas, em vez disso, tem uma estrutura que se apoia em si mesma. A corda de linho fixa a cadeira e lhe dá um acabamento estético. A armação e a base não são fabricadas por separado da lâmina, pelo contrário, ambas são parte da superfície quadrada original. A folha de feltro se dobra e volta a dobrar-se, como um cachecol, criando ao final um objeto que é simultaneamente simétrico e também assimétrico. Com esta cadeira, a forma literalmente segue a função.

NOBODY & LITTLE NOBODY CHAIRS

DESIGN FIRM
KOMPLOT Design

PROJECT MANAGER
James Van Vossel & Tom De Vrieze

PHOTOGRAPHY
Thomas Ibsen, Gunnar Merrild,
Boris Berlin

CLIENT
HAY

NOBODY is produced in one single process by thermopressing a felt mat made of PET polymer fibers. No frame of any kind is used during this process. The production process neither demands any additives such as glues or resins nor any additional materials such as screws or reinforcements. PET felt is a 100 percent recyclable material produced principally from used soda and water bottles. The good air circulation and perfect acoustic properties of PET felt, along with its easiness of cleaning, provide the chair with additional qualities.

FRA
NOBODY est fabriquée par thermomoulage en une seule opération à partir d'une plaque en feutre de fibres polymères PET. Aucune structure d'aucune sorte n'est utilisée au cours du processus, ni d'additif tel que colle ou résine, ni d'autres éléments comme des vis ou des renforts. Le feutre PET est une matière recyclable à 100 % produite principalement à partir de bouteilles d'eau et de soda. Les chaises NOBODY sont légères et empilables. Par ailleurs, le feutre PET présente de nombreux avantages : une bonne circulation de l'air, d'excellentes propriétés acoustiques et une facilité d'entretien.

ESP
NOBODY se fabrica en un solo proceso mediante la termopresión de un tapete de fieltro hecho de fibras de polímero PET. No se utiliza ningún tipo de estructura en este proceso. El proceso de producción tampoco requiere aditivos como colas o resinas ni otros materiales como tornillos o refuerzos. El fieltro de PET es un material 100 % reciclable que se fabrica principalmente con botellas usadas de agua y refrescos. La buena circulación del aire y las perfectas propiedades acústicas del fieltro de PET, así como la facilidad de limpieza, proporcionan a la silla cualidades adicionales.

POR
NOBODY se produz num único processo, através da termo-pressão de uma esteira de feltro, feita de fibras de polímero PET. Não se utiliza nenhum tipo de estrutura durante este processo. O processo de produção não requer nem aditivos como colas ou resinas nem materiais adicionais como parafusos ou reforços. O feltro de PET é um material 100 % reciclável produzido principalmente a partir de garrafas usadas em refrigerantes e água. A boa circulação do ar e as perfeitas propriedades acústicas do feltro de PET, juntamente com sua facilidade de limpeza, proporcionam à cadeira qualidades adicionais.

SPOOK

DESIGN FIRM
ISKOS-BERLIN Design

DESIGNERS
Boris Berlin & Aleksej Iskos

PHOTOGRAPHY
Erik Karlsson & Boris Berlin

CLIENT
Blå Station AB

Design has been preoccupied with the idea of full control over function, form, materials, and so on. Spook is a monoblock chair produced in one single process by thermopressing a felt mat made of PET polymer fibers. No frame of any kind is used during this process. The production process neither demands any additives such as glues or resins nor any additional materials such as screws or reinforcements. PET felt is a 100 percent recyclable material, largely made from used soda and water bottles.

RUBBER STOOL

DESIGN FIRM
h220430

PHOTOGRAPHY
Ikunori Yamamoto

The design team designed a stool made from recycled rubber. Although the stool has a simple frame that consists of bending a single piece of rubber that comprises the seat and legs, which are held in position with bolts, it is incredibly elegant and also comfortable due to the elastic properties of the rubber. The stool can be stored in a small space by rolling it up when it is not in use. We hope that the Rubber Stool becomes widely used as one example of the uses of recycled rubber, and also serves as a trigger for people to realize the deforestation that is taking place to produce natural rubber.

ESP
Hemos diseñado un taburete de caucho reciclado. Aunque el taburete tiene un armazón sencillo que consiste en una pieza de caucho doblado que comprende el asiento y las patas, que se sujetan mediante tornillos, es increíblemente elegante y cómoda debido a las propiedades elásticas del caucho.
El taburete puede guardarse en espacios pequeños enrollándolo cuando no se usa. Confiamos en que el Taburete de caucho se utilice como ejemplo de los usos del caucho reciclado y contribuya a que la gente se dé cuenta de la deforestación que se está llevando a cabo para producir caucho natural.

FRA
Ce matériau recyclé pour fabriquer le tabouret. La structure du tabouret et simple : elle est constituée d'une seule pièce en caoutchouc pliée formant l'assise et les pieds, lesquels sont maintenus par des boulons. Elle n'en est pas moins élégante et confortable grâce aux propriétés élastiques du caoutchouc. Quand on ne s'en sert pas, on peut ranger le tabouret dans un espace réduit en le roulant comme un cylindre.
Nous espérons que le Rubber Stool fera de nombreux adeptes en tant qu'exemple d'utilisation du caoutchouc recyclé, et qu'il servira à attirer l'attention sur le problème de la déforestation causé par la production de caoutchouc naturel.

POR
Projetamos um tamborete feito com borracha reciclada. Embora o tamborete tenha uma estrutura simples, que consiste em dobrar uma só peça de borracha, composta por assento e pernas, que se mantêm no lugar com parafusos, é incrivelmente elegante e também cômoda, devido às propriedades elásticas da borracha. O tamborete pode ser guardado num lugar pequeno, enrolando o mesmo quando não se usa. Esperamos que o Tamborete de borracha seja amplamente tomado como exemplo dos usos da borracha reciclada, e que também sirva como alerta para que as pessoas percebam o desflorestamento que se pratica para a produção da borracha natural.

TRANSIT CHAIRS & TABLES

DESIGN FIRM
Outdoorz Gallery

DESIGNER
Boris Bailly

PHOTOGRAPHY
J.W. Johnson Photography

This transformation of recycled street signs aims to celebrate a raw, American street aesthetic. The unique markings and patina were earned on the road. Created with the precision of Boris Bailly's skills as a sculptor, jeweler, and industrial designer, the pure lines of the chairs and tables perfectly offset the graphics of the recycled signage. Each edge is rounded to a smooth finish. Transit chairs and tables are made individually (based on current signage stock) in Boris'sstudio, andno two pieces are alike. The stainless-steel hardware is rustproof. Recycled champagne corks inserted into the bottom of all chair and table legs protect floors and provide added stability.

FRA

La transformation de panneaux de signalisation célèbre l'esthétique de l'Amérique urbaine : les marques et la patine sont le résultat de leur exposition aux intempéries sur les routes du pays. Les lignes pures des chaises et des tables sont fidèles à la précision légendaire de Boris Bailly, sculpteur, joaillier et dessinateur industriel, et mettent en valeur le graphisme des panneaux recyclés. Chaque arête est abattue pour être lisse au toucher. Chaque chaise et table Transit est fabriquée individuellement (suivant les panneaux en stock) dans le studio de Boris, et il n'y en a pas deux pareilles. Le matériau, qui est de l'acier inoxydable, ne rouille pas. Des bouchons de champagne recyclés sont utilisés comme patins pour les pieds de toutes les chaises et tables, pour protéger les planchers et procurer une plus grande stabilité.

ESP

Esta transformación de señales de tráfico recicladas tiene como objetivo celebrar una estética callejera norteamericana en estado puro. El lustre y las marcas únicas que ostentan se han obtenido en la carretera. Gracias a las habilidades de Boris Bailly como escultor, orfebre y diseñador industrial, las líneas puras de las sillas y las mesas equilibran a la perfección los gráficos de las señales recicladas. Los bordes se redondean hasta que se obtiene un acabado suave. Las sillas y las mesas de tráfico se fabrican individualmente (en función de las señales disponibles) en el estudio de Boris, de manera que no hay dos piezas iguales. Son de acero inoxidable. Los tapones reciclados de botellas de champán que se insertan en los extremos de las patas de todas las sillas y las mesas protegen las superficies y proporcionan una estabilidad añadida.

POR

Esta transformação de sinais de trânsito reciclados tem por objetivo realizar uma estética de rua americana em estado puro. As marcas singulares e sua pátina foram adquiridas na estrada. Criadas com a precisão das habilidades de Boris Bailly como escultor, joalheiro e Designer industrial, as linhas puras das cadeiras e mesas compensam perfeitamente os gráficos dos sinais reciclados. Cada canto é arredondado para um acabamento suave. As cadeiras e mesas de tráfego são feitas individualmente (com base nos sinais disponíveis) no estúdio de Boris, e não há duas peças iguais. O material de aço inoxidável é à prova de oxidação. As rolhas recicladas de champanhe, inseridas na ponta das pernas de todas as cadeiras e mesas, protegem o piso e proporcionam uma estabilidade adicional.

RECYCLED FOAM SOFT PAD COUCH AND ARMCHAIR

DESIGN FIRM
Stephan Schulz Studio

DESIGNER
Stephan Schulz

PHOTOGRAPHY
Matthias Ritzmann

CLIENT
Prototyp

The couch and armchairs are made out of recycled foam. Their natural and colorful shape stems from their distinctive hackled-foam source material. The system consists of the basic elements of two different panels that can be easily connected together with a simple cable-control framework. By connecting the panels you can easily achieve a wide diversity of couch and sofa versions.

ESP
El sofá y los sillones son de espuma reciclada. La forma natural y colorida se debe a la característica espuma acuchillada. El conjunto consta de los elementos básicos de dos paneles que se conectan fácilmente mediante una sencilla estructura controlada por cables. Al conectar los paneles se obtiene una amplia gama de combinaciones de sofá y sillón.

FRA
Le canapé et le fauteuil sont en mousse recyclée. Leur forme naturelle et colorée est due au matériau lui-même. Le système est constitué des éléments de base de deux types de blocs qui peuvent être facilement reliés entre eux au moyen d'une simple structure en câbles réglables. On peut assembler les blocs de diverses façons pour obtenir une grande variété de canapés.

POR
O sofá e as poltronas são feitos de espuma reciclada. Sua forma natural e colorida é proveniente da característica espuma triturada. O sistema é composto pelos elementos básicos de dois painéis diferentes, que podem conectar-se facilmente com uma simples estrutura controlada por cabos. Ao conectar os painéis, você pode conseguir facilmente uma vasta gama de versões de sofá e poltrona.

LATEX ROLL

DESIGN FIRM
13 ricrea

DESIGNERS
Angela Mensi, Ingrid Taro & Cristina Merlo

PHOTOGRAPHY
Francesco Arena

The temporary indoor seats in this series are available in different colors. The seats are made using cut offs from the shoe industry. The latex rolls are fastened with plastic belts. Each seat weighs about five kilograms.

FRA
Les sièges d'intérieur d'appoint de cette série existent en différentes couleurs. Ils sont fabriqués à partir de chutes de l'industrie de la chaussure. Les rouleaux en latex sont attachés avec des ceintures en plastique. Chaque siège pèse environ cinq kilos.

POR
Os assentos de interior temporários nesta série estão disponíveis em diferentes cores. Os assentos são feitos usando retalhos da indústria de calçados. Os rolos de látex são fixados com cintos de plástico. Cada assento pesa uns cinco quilos.

ESP
Los asientos temporales de interior de esta serie están disponibles en diferentes colores. Los asientos están hechos de retales procedentes de la industria del calzado. Los rollos de látex se sujetan mediante tiras de plástico. Cada asiento pesa unos cinco kilos.

POUF DE PAILLE

DESIGNER
Tetê Knecht

PHOTOGRAPHY
Andrés Otero

CLIENT
Galerie Slott

These pouffes are a combination of straw and latex, a mixture that creates a smooth and very comfortable surface that is also durable. For this project, Tété Knecht focused on one principle: combining a dry material with a wet one to create something new. Combining organic material with industrial leftovers, Knecht mixed materials such as coal, plastic, straw, metal, carbon, and fiberglass flowers with glue, latex, silicone, and resin.

FRA
Ces poufs sont fabriqués dans une matière associant paille et latex. Le résultat est une surface douce et confortable, qui a aussi l'avantage d'être durable. Pour ce projet, Tété Knecht s'est concentré sur un principe : combiner un matériau sec à un autre humide pour créer quelque chose de nouveau. Pour assembler un matériau organique à des surplus industriels, Knecht a mélangé des matières telles que charbon, plastique, paille, métal, carbone et pot de fleurs en fibres de verre avec de la colle, du latex, de la silicone et de la résine.

ESP
Estos pufs son una combinación de paja y látex, una mezcla que resulta en una superficie suave y sumamente confortable, además de duradera. Para este proyecto Tété Knecht se basó en un principio: combinar un material seco con uno húmedo para crear algo nuevo. Aunando materiales orgánicos con desechos industriales, Knecht mezcló materiales tales como carbón, plástico, paja, metal, carbono y flores de fibra de vidrio con cola, silicona y resina.

POR
Estes Puff são uma combinação de palha e látex, uma mistura que cria uma superfície suave e muito cômoda, e também duradoura. Para este projeto, Tété Knecht centrou-se num princípio: combinar um material seco com um úmido para criar algo novo. Combinando matéria orgânica com resíduos industriais, Knecht misturou materiais como carvão, plástico, palha, metal, carbono e flores de fibra de vidro com cola, silicone e resina.

INCASSO DURABLE FURNITURE

DESIGN FIRM
Fermin Guerrero

DESIGNER
Fermin Guerrero

PHOTOGRAPHY
Tammara Leites & Fermin Guerrero

Attractive and with a low environmental impact, this furniture set is the result of the efficient reuse of cardboard tubes that were originally used as spools for Tetra Pak rolls. Incasso was born as a response to the problem of different companies discarding these tubes. The chairs and the table are both assembled using small cuts in the tubes, eliminating the need for extra materials for the joints. The range's environmental footprint is therefore reduced and the raw material is optimally employed.

Cet ensemble esthétique et à faible impact environnemental est le résultat d'un réemploi efficace de bobines en cartons provenant de rouleaux de briques alimentaires. Incasso a été conçu pour répondre au problème de gestion de ces déchets produits par différentes sociétés. Les éléments des chaises et de la table s'emboîtent grâce à des petites incisions pratiquées directement dans le carton. Aucun autre matériel n'est requis pour réaliser le montage. L'empreinte écologique de la gamme Incasso est minime, le matériau brut étant utilisé de manière optimale.

Atraente e com um baixo impacto ambiental, este conjunto de móveis é o resultado da reutilização eficiente de tubos de papelão, que originalmente foram usados como bobinas para rolos de Tetra Pak. Incasso nasceu como resposta ao problema de diversas empresas que jogavam fora estes tubos. As cadeiras e a mesa foram montadas fazendo pequenos cortes nos tubos, eliminando a necessidade de materiais extras para as junções. Deste modo, a pegada ambiental da faixa se reduz e a matéria-prima se utiliza de forma otimizada.

Atractivo y con escaso impacto en el medioambiente, este conjunto de muebles es el resultado de la reutilización eficiente de tubos de cartón, que se habían empleado anteriormente como bobinas para rollos de Tetra Pak. Incasso nació como solución al problema de las numerosas empresas que desechan estos tubos. Las sillas y la mesa se montan gracias a los pequeños cortes en los tubos, eliminándose la necesidad de materiales adicionales para las junturas. De este modo disminuye la huella medioambiental de la gama y la materia prima se emplea de manera óptima.

ANNIE THE SHOPPING TROLLEY CHAIR

DESIGN FIRM
reestore.com

DESIGNER
Max McMurdo

Annie the Shopping Trolley Chair is produced from a salvaged shopping trolley. These trolleys are typically scrapped due to wonky wheels, but reestore transforms them into beautiful upright chairs for the home or office. Annie the Shopping Trolley Chair can be upholstered in your choice of fabric and powder coated to your specification in any color.

ESP
La silla de carrito Annie está hecha con un carrito de la compra recuperado. Estos carritos suelen desecharse cuando se tuercen las ruedas, pero reestore los ha transformado en preciosas sillas de respaldo recto para la casa o la oficina. La silla de carrito Annie se puede tapizar con la tela que prefiera y pintar con la pintura electrostática que más le guste.

FRA
Le fauteuil Annie the Shopping Trolley est fabriqué à partir d'un caddie de supermarché de récupération. En général, les caddies sont envoyés à la casse en raison de roulettes défectueuses. reestore les transforme en superbes fauteuils droits, à leur place aussi bien à la maison qu'au bureau. Le fauteuil peut être recouvert du tissu de votre choix et peint dans la couleur de vos rêves.

POR
Annie, a cadeira do carrinho de compras, foi produzida a partir de um carrinho de compras recuperado. Estes carrinhos, normalmente, são rejeitados em função de suas rodas ficarem tortas, mas reestore os transforma em preciosas cadeiras verticais para o lar ou para o escritório. Annie, a cadeira do carrinho de compras, pode ser estofada com o tecido da sua escolha e pode ser pintado a seu gosto, com pintura eletrostática.

MAX THE BATH TUB CHAISE

DESIGN FIRM
reestore.com

DESIGNER
Max McMurdo

Max the Bath Tub Chaise is a contemporary twist on the sofa that briefly featured in *Breakfast at Tiffany's*. Created from a vintage, cast-iron bath tub and upholstered in the fabric of your choice, Max the Bath Tub Chaise is perfectly formed for single-seat slouching or as a sofa for two.

ESP
El diván de bañera Max es una interpretación contemporánea del sofá que apareció brevemente en *Desayuno con diamantes*. Creado a partir de una antigua bañera de hierro forjado y tapizado con la tela que prefiera, el diván de bañera Max está perfectamente formado para usarlo como tumbona para uno o sofá para dos.

FRA
La causeuse Max the Bath Tub est un clin d'œil au canapé que l'on ne voit qu'un instant dans le film *Breakfast at Tiffany's*. Créé à partir d'une baignoire d'époque en fonte et recouvert du tissu de votre choix, la causeuse Max the Bath Tub est le siège parfait pour faire la sieste en solo ou s'assoire en duo.

POR
Max, o divã de banheira, é uma variação contemporânea do sofá que saiu brevemente em *Café da manhã no Tiffany's*. Criado a partir de uma antiga banheira de ferro forjado e estofado no tecido de sua escolha Max, o divã de banheira, está perfeitamente configurado para que uma só pessoa relaxe ou como sofá para dois.

SILVANA THE WASH DRUM TABLE

DESIGN FIRM
reestore

DESIGNER
Max McMurdo

Reestore's brightest young talent is Silvana. Casting beams of light from an eco-friendly lightbulb, she produces a beautiful ambient glow that shows off her polished, stainless-steel, wash-drum body. She is finished with a new, frosted-glass surface for mug-resting heaven.

ESP
Silvana es el talento más joven y brillante de reestore. Gracias a la luz que arroja una bombilla ecológica, emite un hermoso brillo ambiental que resalta el reluciente cuerpo de acero inoxidable de un tambor de lavadora. Presenta un acabado con una nueva superficie de cristal esmerilado idónea para las tazas.

FRA
Silvana est la petite dernière de reestore, aussi douée que radieuse. Elle diffuse des rayons de lumière émanant d'une ampoule basse consommation, et produit une lumière d'ambiance chaleureuse qui met en valeur l'acier inoxydable poli de son corps de tambour de machine à laver. Comme finition, elle dispose d'une plaque en verre dépoli qui accueillera verres et tasses avec bonheur.

POR
O talento mais jovem e brilhante de Reestore é Silvana. Lançando raios de luz de uma lâmpada ecológica, produz um bonito brilho ambiental que realça o corpo polido de aço inoxidável do tambor de uma máquina de lavar. Recebe como acabamento uma nova superfície de vidro esmerilado como céu para as xícaras.

BACK IN THE SADDLE

DESIGN FIRM
Lula Dot

DESIGNER
Lucy Norman

CLIENT
North South Ideas Gallery

This seat, commissioned by North South Ideas Gallery for their bicycle show in Highgate, London, is made from old bicycle saddles collected from all the bike shops in and around the Hackney area of London. The saddles' seat posts are positioned around two used bicycle wheels.

ESP
Este asiento, encargado por North South Ideas Gallery para la feria ciclista de High-gate, Londres, se compone de viejos sillines obtenidos en todas las tiendas de bicicletas del barrio londinenses de Hackney y sus alrededores. Las barras del sillín se colocan alrededor de dos ruedas de bicicleta usadas.

FRA
Ce tabouret est une œuvre de commande de North South Ideas Gallery destiné à leur exposition de bicyclettes de Highgate, Londres. Il est créé à partir de vieilles selles de vélos récupérées dans les magasins de bicyclettes du quartier londonien de Hackney et de ses environs. Les tubes des différentes selles sont fixés autour de deux vieilles roues de bicyclettes.

POR
Este assento, encomendado por North South Ideias Gallery para a Feira da bicicleta em Highgate, Londres, é feito de velhos selins de bicicleta recolhidos em todas as lojas de bicicletas da zona de Hackney (Londres) e de seus arredores. Os tubos do selim são colocados em volta de duas rodas usadas de bicicleta.

PUFFY, TIED & TIRED

DESIGNER
Maria Westerberg

PHOTOGRAPHY
Maria Westerberg

This unique piece is made from a large tractor tire covered with 149 vintage silk ties. The quality of silk makes it feel luxurious and the different colors and patterns of the ties are dynamic and unique. Puffy, Tied & Tired can be used as a piece of social furniture on which as many as six people can sit together, or if the mood is not social the seat's users can have their backs to one another. Since the inside is a tire filled with air, the size can be minimized in transport. The ecological idea is to make use of existing ties that are exchangeable and an existing tire that can be easily transported when deflated.

FRA
Ce pouf original est créé à partir d'une chambre à air de tracteur recouverte de 149 cravates vintage en soie. La qualité de la soie invite au luxe et au confort, les couleurs et les motifs variés conférant une dynamique unique à l'ensemble. L'idée ici est de tirer parti de ces cravates et de les rendre belles dans un nouveau contexte. Le pouf Puffy, Tied & Tired est un siège qui invite à la conversation puisque six personnes peuvent s'assoire dessus en même temps. Si le moment n'est pas favorable aux échanges, les personnes peuvent se tourner le dos. Le pouf peut être transporté très facilement en dégonflant la chambre à air. Le principe écologique est double : on emploie des cravates que l'on possède déjà et que l'on peut facilement remplacer, et une chambre à air de tracteur que l'on peut dégonfler pour le transport.

ESP
Esta pieza única está hecha con una rueda de tractor de gran tamaño cubierta con 149 corbatas de seda antiguas. La calidad de la seda hace que tenga una superficie suntuosa, y los diferentes colores y estampados de las corbatas son dinámicos y únicos. La rueda corbatero puede usarse como mueble de fiesta, pues da cabida hasta a seis personas, y si el ambiente no invita a la conversación, los usuarios pueden darse la espalda. Como el interior es un neumático lleno de aire, el tamaño se puede minimizar para su transporte. La idea ecológica es emplear corbatas existentes, que son intercambiables, y un neumático, que puede transportarse fácilmente cuando se deshincha.

POR
Esta peça única é feita com um grande pneu de trator coberto com 149 antigas gravatas de seda. A qualidade da seda faz com que o tato seja luxuoso, e as diferentes cores e estampados das gravatas sejam dinâmicos e únicos. O Inchado, "corbateado" e "neumaticado" pode ser usado como móvel social, no qual podem sentar-se até 6 pessoas juntas ou, se o ambiente não é social, os usuários podem sentar-se virando as costas uns para os outros. Como o interior é um pneu cheio de ar, o tamanho se pode minimizar para o seu transporte. A ideia ecológica é fazer uso de gravatas existentes, que são permutáveis, e um pneu existente, que se pode transportar facilmente quando se esvazia.

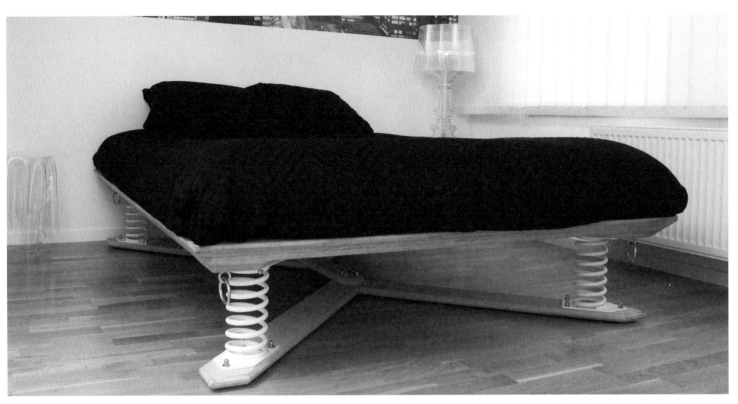

SPRING BED

DESIGN FIRM
TH Design

PROJECT MANAGER
Thor Høy

PHOTOGRAPHY
Cph Mass

The Spring Bed is a plywood construction with a slatted frame. The springs ensure a comfortably responding support irrespective of the hardness of the mattress. Your bed partner and the bed itself can easily move around without waking you up. For added fun the corners of the bed are supplied with sturdy eyebolts with steel rings, which can also be used for the practical purpose of hoisting the bed through a window. The springs come from an old, discarded Ford Escort.

FRA

Le lit Spring Bed est une structure en contreplaqué multiplis. Les ressorts assurent un excellent confort, indépendamment de la dureté du matelas qui repose sur une surface lattée. La personne qui partage votre lit peut bouger ou déplacer ce dernier sans vous réveiller. Des anneaux très solides sont placés aux quatre coins. Ils sont aussi esthétiques que pratiques puisqu'on peut s'en servir pour hisser le lit par la fenêtre quand on emménage. Les ressorts ont été récupérés dans une vieille Ford Escort trouvée à la casse.

ESP

A cama de molas é uma construção de chapas compensadas com uma estrutura de ripas. As molas garantem um suporte cômodo, independentemente da dureza do colchão. Seu companheiro de cama e a própria cama se podem mover facilmente sem o despertar. Para ficar mais divertido, as esquinas da cama são equipadas com robustas argolas com anéis de aço, que também podem ser usados para subir a cama através de uma janela. As molas são de um velho Ford Escort rejeitado.

POR

La cama de muelles consiste en una construcción de madera contrachapada con un somier de listones. Los muelles aseguran un soporte cómodo, independientemente de la firmeza del colchón. Su pareja y hasta la propia cama pueden moverse fácilmente sin despertarlo. Para más diversión, las esquinas de la cama disponen de gruesas argollas con anillas de acero que también pueden usarse para introducirla a través de una ventana. Los muelles proceden de un viejo Ford Escort desechado.

RE:COVER

DESIGN FIRM
Studio Fredrik Färg

PHOTOGRAPHY
Studio Fredrik Färg

DESIGNER
Fredrik Färg

RE:cover is a set of old chairs with new covers made from 100 percent recyclable polyester felt. Fredrik takes his inspiration from classic tailoring that never goes out of style, such as suits and dinner jackets. By using old chairs from flea markets, removing the back rest, and replacing it with a new textile covering/structure of moldable polyester felt, he is creating "slow-fashion" furniture and giving old chairs a new look.

FRA
RE:cover est un ensemble de vieilles chaises équipées d'un dossier neuf en feutre polyester 100 % recyclable dont la forme s'inspire des vêtements classiques tels que le costume et le smoking. Fredrik récupère de vieilles chaises dans des marchés aux puces, démonte leur dossier et les remplace par une nouvelle structure moulée recouverte d'un tissu en feutre polyester. Il crée ainsi des meubles « néodesign » et redonne vie à des chaises anciennes.

ESP
RE:cover es un conjunto de sillas viejas equipadas con fundas nuevas de fieltro de poliéster 100 % reciclable. Fredrik se ha inspirado en las confecciones clásicas que nunca pasan de moda, como los trajes y los esmóquines. Empleando sillas viejas obtenidas en mercadillos a las que ha quitado el respaldo, reemplazándolo con una nueva funda o estructura de fieltro de poliéster maleable, Fredrik ha creado muebles "lentos" al tiempo que insuflaba un aire nuevo a estas viejas sillas.

POR
RE:cover é um conjunto de velhas cadeiras com capas novas feitas com feltro de poliéster 100 % reciclável. Fredrik se inspira numa confecção clássica que nunca passa de moda, como os ternos e os smokings. Ao usar velhas cadeiras de feiras, tirar o apoio e substituir o mesmo com uma nova estrutura ou cobertura têxtil de feltro de poliéster modelável, Fredrik cria móveis de moda slow e dá um novo ar às cadeiras velhas.

RIP + TATTER KID'S CHAIR

DESIGN FIRM
Pete Oyler Design

DESIGNER
Pete Oyler

PHOTOGRAPHY
Matthew Williams

Sculpted by hammering out industrial cardboard, the Rip + Tatter Kid's Chair is 100 percent recyclable. Non-toxic, durable, and full of energy, the chair can also be taken out with the rest of the recycling when the time comes.

FRA
Le fauteuil pour enfant Rip + Tatter créé à partir de carton industriel embouti est 100 % recyclable. Non toxique, durable et plein d'énergie, ce fauteuil peut aller dans le bac de déchets recyclables lorsqu'il aura fait son temps.

ESP
Esculpida con cartón industrial, la silla infantil Rip + Tatter es 100 % reciclable. La propia silla, atóxica, duradera y rebosante de energía, también puede reciclarse cuando llegue el momento.

POR
Esculpida trabalhando papelão industrial, a cadeira infantil Rip + Tatter é 100 % reciclável. Não tóxica, durável e cheia de energia a cadeira poderá também ser reciclada quando chegar o momento.

THREE LITTLE PIGS

DESIGN FIRM
Sanserif Creatius

DESIGNERS
Ana Yago & José Antonio Giménez

PHOTOGRAPHY
Eduardo Peris

CLIENT
El Corte Inglés, Grupo La Plana,
Feria Hábitat Valencia, AFCO

These pieces of furniture are made from 100 percent biodegradable corrugated cardboard. Their functional, economical, and serialized production is based on a single die. Auxiliary processes are reduced to the production of the assembly unit, whilet he costs, environmental impact, and the collateral energy consumption used in production are similarly reduced. And, of course, screws, wedges, and the like are not used. Compression tests indicate that the range has an estimated resistance of one thousand kilograms. The idea behind the collection is to show people the importance of materials such as cardboard that until now had never even been seriously considered for the home. Based on the popular children's story of the same name, Three Little Pigs is a fable about the importance of the materials with which we create our everyday habitat growth.

FRA
Ces pièces de mobilier sont fabriquées en carton ondulé 100 % biodégradable. Leur production fonctionnelle, économique et en série s'effectue à partir d'un moule unique. Les autres étapes se limitent à la chaîne de montage, ce qui réduit les coûts, l'incidence sur l'environnement et l'énergie consommée lors de leur fabrication. Par ailleurs, les meubles n'utilisent aucune vis, boulon, coin ou autre. Les essais de résistance à la pression montrent qu'ils supportent jusqu'à une tonne.
L'idée de la collection est de montrer aux gens l'importance de matériaux tels que le carton qui jusqu'à présent n'ont pas vraiment été exploités pour le mobilier d'intérieur. Elle s'inspire du conte des Trois petits cochons, qui est une fable sur l'importance des matériaux que nous utilisons pour créer notre habitat de tous les jours.

ESP
Estos muebles están elaborados con cartón ondulado 100 % biodegradable. Se fabrican en serie, de una forma funcional y económica con un solo troquel. Los procesos auxiliares se reducen a la fabricación de la unidad de montaje, al tiempo que los costes, el impacto en el medio ambiente y el consumo colateral de energía durante la producción también disminuyen. Además, claro está, no se usan tornillos, cuñas ni herramientas similares. Las pruebas de compresión han indicado una resistencia aproximada de una tonelada. La idea de esta colección es enseñarle al público la importancia de materiales como el cartón, que hasta el momento no se han tenido en cuenta en el ámbito doméstico. Basado en el famoso cuento del mismo título, Los tres cerditos es una fábula sobre la importancia de los materiales con los que creamos nuestro hábitat cotidiano.

POR
Estes móveis são feitos de papelão canelado 100 % biodegradável. Sua produção funcional, econômica, e em série baseia-se numa única matriz. Os processos auxiliares reduzem-se à produção da unidade de montagem, ao mesmo tempo que os custos, o impacto ambiental e o consumo colateral de energia usados na produção também se reduzem. E, claro está, não se usam nem parafusos, nem cunhas nem outros elementos semelhantes. Os testes de compressão indicam que a faixa tem uma resistência estimada de mil quilos.
A ideia da coleção é mostrar às pessoas a importância de materiais como o papelão, cujo uso para o lar até o momento não foi seriamente considerado. Baseado no popular conto infantil do mesmo título, Os três porquinhos é uma fábula sobre a importância dos materiais com os quais criamos nosso habitat cotidiano.

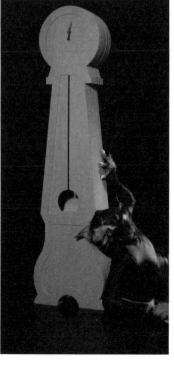

PAPTON

DESIGN FIRM
FUCHS + FUNKE

DESIGNERS
Kai Funke & Wilm Fuchs

PHOTOGRAPHY
FUCHS + FUNKE

As simple as a paper plane in its design, a few folds transform a composite panel into a lightweight chair. The structure is based on dividing panels into load-bearing areas and bending zones. Low weight and volume allow a large quantity of unfolded chairs to be stored and transported in a dense package. The chair owes its characteristic shape to a simple pattern, with just a couple of polygons creating a clear, graphic unity. Its optical lightness and dynamism stem from its open structure. Instead of generating a massive, monolithic look, a vivid, monoplanar quality is achieved.

FRA

Aussi simple dans sa forme qu'une cocotte en papier, quelques plis suffisent à transformer un panneau composite en chaise aérienne. La structure est formée de zones porteusesa et de points de pliages. Comme les chaises sont légères et de faible encombrement, on peut en empiler une grande quantité pour les ranger ou les transporter sous forme de paquet compact. La chaise se caractérise par une forme simple combinant plusieurs polygones qui constituent un ensemble à la fois sobre et élégante. La structure ouverte produit un effet de légèreté et de dynamisme. Loin d'être massive ou monolithique, la chaise Papton est aérienne et esthétique.

ESP

Con un diseño tan sencillo como el de un avión de papel, mediante unos pocos pliegues se transforma un panel de conglomerado en una silla ligera. La estructura se basa en la división de los paneles en secciones de carga y secciones flexibles. Como las sillas abiertas son ligeras y abultan poco, puede guardarse y transportarse un gran número de ellas en un solo paquete. La característica forma de la silla obedece a un patrón sencillo, en el que se obtiene una unidad gráfica definida mediante dos polígonos. Su ligereza óptica y su dinamismo se deben a su estructura abierta. En vez de causar una impresión robusta y monolítica, se consigue una imagen monoplana.

POR

Tão simples como um avião de papel em seu design, algumas dobras transformam um painel composto numa cadeira leve. A estrutura baseia-se em dividir painéis em zonas que suportam peso e zonas para se reclinar. O baixo peso e baixo volume permitem que sejam armazenadas e transportadas muitas cadeiras sem dobrar, num único pacote de carga. A cadeira deve sua forma característica a um padrão simples, com um par de polígonos que criam uma unidade gráfica precisa. Sua leveza visual e seu dinamismo brotam de sua estrutura aberta. Em vez de causar uma impressão maciça e monolítica, consegue-se uma característica de plano único.

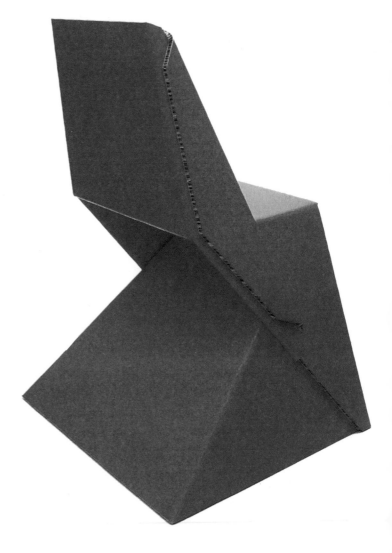

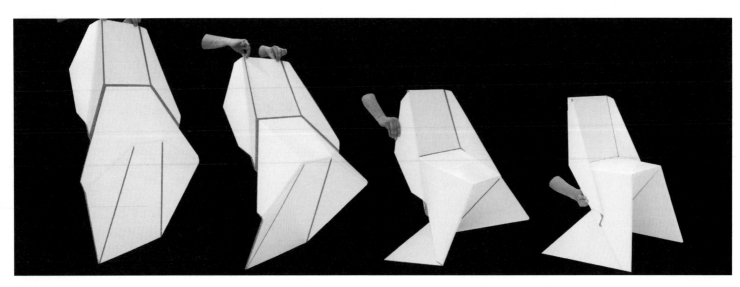

PIAO-PAPER CHAIR

DESIGN FIRM
Hangzhou PINWU Design Studio

DESIGNERS
Christoph John, Zhang Lei,
Jovana Bogdanovic

PHOTOGRAPHY
Zhang Shensen

The idea for this paper chair came from the way the paper covering of a traditional Chinese umbrella is attached to its framework. The natural and very durable paper is glued directly to the bamboo rods. The seat of the chair also takes advantage of this material's characteristics. The combination of numerous glued layers of paper and the rounded shape creates a stable and solid form with a hint of flexibility. The base construction is made of solid beech. A thin coating of natural wax protects the paper from water and other potentially damaging materials, allowing the natural appearance and feel of the paper to be preserved. The rough edge of the chair emphasizes the natural structure of handmade paper and contrasts with the pure shape of the main shell.

FRA

L'idée de cette chaise repose sur la façon dont le papier des ombrelles chinoises traditionnelles est fixé à leur cadre. Le papier naturel très résistant est collé directement sur les baleines en bambou. Les différentes couches de papier collées et la forme ronde produisent une structure solide et stable non dénuée d'une certaine souplesse. La base et les pieds sont en bouleau massif. Une fine couche de cire naturelle protège le papier contre l'eau et d'autres agents potentiellement agressifs, tout en préservant son aspect et sa texture naturels. La finition grossière des bords du fauteuil renforce la structure naturelle du papier fabriqué à la main et contraste avec la forme pure de la coquille.

ESP

La idea de esta silla de papel surgió del modo en el que el papel de las sombrillas tradicionales chinas se adhieren a la estructura de estas. El papel, natural y muy duradero, se encola directamente al bastón de bambú. El asiento de la silla también aprovecha las características de este material. Gracias a la combinación de numerosas capas de papel pegadas y la forma redondeada se obtiene una figura estable y firme, aunque con un aire flexible. La construcción básica es de haya robusta. Una fina capa de cera natural protege el papel del agua y otros materiales que podrían deteriorarlo, al tiempo que se conserva la apariencia natural y el tacto del papel. El contorno irregular de la silla enfatiza la estructura natural del papel hecho a mano y contrasta con la forma pura del armazón.

POR

A ideia desta cadeira de papel surgiu do modo como é fixado à sua estrutura o papel que cobre uma tradicional sombrinha chinesa. O papel, natural e muito durável, cola-se diretamente à vara de bambu. O assento da cadeira também tira vantagem das características deste material. A combinação das diversas camadas coladas de papel com a forma arredondada cria uma figura estável e sólida com um toque de flexibilidade. A construção básica é feita de faia sólida. Uma fina cobertura de cera natural protege o papel da água e de outros materiais potencialmente prejudiciais, permitindo que se conserve a aparência natural e o tato do papel. A borda irregular da cadeira enfatiza a estrutura natural de papel feito à mão e contrasta com a forma pura da carapaça principal.

CHAIR 4A

DESIGN FIRM
Michael Young Ltd

DESIGNERS
Michael Young

CLIENT
Hip restaurant group SML

Michael Young designed Chair-4a as part of his extended Works in China collection. Chair-4a wascreated as part of the interiors for Alexi Robinson's hip restaurant group SML. The project explores new technologies and typologies made available only by working with highly skilled engineering facilities in Shenzhen, China. According to Young, developing the chair came about after "I realized that if I could capture the engineering skills employed by local industry and put that depth of knowledge in aluminum research in furniture design using a similar mass-produced nature, I could design a state-of-the-art and relevant chair. In recent years chairs have taken all nature of shape and form due to the use of plastics, but plastic in itself is not a pleasant material to use. Its tactility and its aging process are highly unpleasant. For the same price I can use recycled aluminum and in fact create a more sustainable chair that also creates jobs rather than having a man just pressing a button. The tooling is complex but we created a chair that lasts a lifetime, engineered beyond plastic technology and far more sustainable." Chair-4a comes in a number of different finishes including leather seat inserts and floor pegs. The chair, Young concludes, "pays homage to all the things I love."

FRA
La chaise Chair-4a fait partie de la collection étendue « Works in China » de Michael Young. Elle a été créée pour l'aménagement intérieur du restaurant branché d'Alexi Robinson du groupe SML. Le projet exploite de nouvelles technologies et typologies qui ne sont disponibles que dans les centres d'ingénierie dernier cri de Shenzhen en Chine. Young nous raconte comment l'idée de la chaise lui est venue : « J'ai pensé que si je pouvais tirer parti des avancées de l'industrie mécanique locale pour approfondir les recherches sur l'aluminium et les appliquer à la conception de meubles produits en série, je pourrais créer une chaise à la fois ultramoderne et confortable. Ces dernières années, on a vu apparaître sur le marché des chaises aux formes les plus variées grâce aux possibilités du plastique, mais ce matériau en soi n'est pas très plaisant à utiliser. Il est désagréable au toucher et vieillit très mal. Pour le même prix, je peux recycler de l'aluminium et créer une chaise bien plus écologique qui génère des emplois au lieu d'avoir juste une personne qui appuie sur un bouton. La fabrication est complexe, mais grâce à une technologie plus avancée que celle du plastique, nous avons créé une chaise bien plus écologique qui dure pour toute la vie. Chair-4a est disponible dans différentes finitions, dont les détails en cuir et les patins.

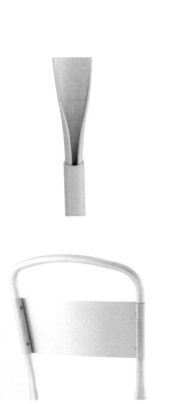

ESP

Michael Young diseñó la silla 4a en el contexto de la colección "Obras en China", donde formaba parte de los interiores para SML, el conglomerado de restaurantes de moda de Alexi Robinson. El proyecto explora nuevas tecnologías y tipologías que solo se encuentran disponibles cuando se trabaja con las instalaciones de ingeniería especializadas de Shenzhen, China. Según Young, la silla se le ocurrió cuando "me di cuenta de que si capturaba los métodos de ingeniería que empleaban las industrias locales y aplicaba esos conocimientos a la investigación del aluminio para el diseño de mobiliario, utilizando la misma fabricación en masa, diseñaría una silla de vanguardia. En los últimos años las sillas han adoptado todo tipo de estados y formas debido al uso de plástico, pero no es fácil trabajar con plástico. La textura y el proceso de envejecimiento son sumamente desagradables. Por el mismo precio, puedo usar aluminio reciclado y diseñar una silla más sostenible que además crea empleo, en lugar de que una sola persona apriete un botòn. El torneado es complejo, pero hemos creado una silla para toda la vida, que supera a la tecnología del plástico y es mucho más sostenible." La silla 4a está disponible con diferentes acabados, incluyendo asientos de cuero y soportes para el suelo. La silla, concluye Young, "es un homenaje a todas las cosas que amo."

POR

Michael Young projetou a cadeira 4a como parte de suas Obras ampliadas na coleção China. A cadeira 4a foi criada como parte dos interiores para o grupo SML, restaurantes de moda de Alexi Robinson. O projeto explora novas tecnologias e tipologias somente disponíveis ao trabalhar com instalações de engenharia muito especializada em Shenzhen, China. Conforme Young, o desenvolvimento da cadeira ocorreu depois de que "percebi que se fosse possível captar o potencial de engenharia utilizado na indústria local e usar no projeto de móveis toda essa profundidade de conhecimentos da pesquisa do alumínio, utilizando uma natureza semelhante produzida em massa, então poderia projetar uma importante cadeira de vanguarda. Nos últimos anos, as cadeiras ganharam todo tipo de estados e formas devido ao uso de plástico, mas o plástico em si mesmo não é um material agradável de se usar. Sua textura e seu processo de envelhecimento são muito desagradáveis. Pelo mesmo preço, posso usar alumínio reciclado e criar, de fato, uma cadeira mais sustentável que também cria empregos, em vez de ter uma única pessoa apertando um botão. O torneamento é complicado, mas criamos uma cadeira que dura a vida inteira, projetada mais à frente da tecnologia do plástico e muito mais sustentável." A cadeira 4a é oferecida em diversos acabamentos, incluindo inserções de pele no assento e fixações para o piso. A cadeira, conclui Young, "homenageia todas as coisas que amo".

THE RUBENS COLLECTION (MADAM RUBENS, PLUS DE MADAM RUBENS, PETIT POUF)

DESIGN FIRM
Studio Frank Willems

DESIGNER
Frank Willems

PHOTOGRAPHY
Frank Willems

Willems's inspiration for this collection came from visiting a waste-processing facility while carrying out a research project on extending the life of various types of waste, during which he discovered that almost all types of waste appeared to have a destination, except mattresses. A bulky, comfortable seat is created by folding discarded mattresses. The sexy legs are the result of dismantling a discarded stool. By folding the mattresses differently and using an assortment of chair legs, every single lady is unique, just like they ought to be. After being coated the seats of the Rubens collection are fresh, hygienic, and totally rejuvenated. There are two ways of folding the mattresses, which create a compact version and an asymmetrical version.

FRA
L'idée de cette collection est venue à Willems le jour où il a visité une usine de traitement de déchets. Il travaillait sur un projet de recherche sur la manière d'allonger la durée de vie de différents types de déchets et s'est rendu compte que pratiquement tous avaient un usage, sauf les matelas. Pour créer une chaise confortable, on plie un matelas mis au rebut. Pour fabriquer les pieds, on utilise les éléments d'un tabouret jeté aux ordures. Comme les matelas sont pliés de différentes façons et qu'il existe une grande variété de pieds, chaque Madam et Plus de Madam est unique. Grâce à leur nouveau revêtement, les sièges de la collection Rubens sont propres, hygiéniques et complètement rajeunis. Il existe deux manières de plier les matelas : on obtient ainsi soit une version compact, soit une version asymétrique.

ESP
Willem encontró la inspiración para esta colección durante una visita a una planta procesadora de basura donde descubrió que casi todos los residuos se destinaban a algún fin, excepto los colchones. Al doblar los colchones desechados obtenemos un asiento confortable y voluminoso. Las sensuales patas proceden de taburetes viejos desmontados. Puesto que los colchones están doblados de distintas maneras y se emplea un surtido de patas, cada versión es única, como debe ser. Con una capa de pintura, los asientos de la colección Rubens se presentan frescos, higiénicos y totalmente rejuvenecidos. Los colchones se doblan de dos maneras, obteniéndose una versión compacta y otra asimétrica.

POR
A inspiração de Willem para esta coleção surgiu ao visitar uma instalação processadora de resíduos, quando realizava um projeto de pesquisa para ampliar a vida útil de diversos tipos de resíduos, durante a qual descobriu que quase todos os tipos de resíduos pareciam ter um destino, exceto os colchões. Cria-se um assento cômodo e volumoso dobrando colchões descartados. As pernas sexy são o resultado de desmantelar um tamborete descartado. Dobrando os colchões de forma diferente e usando um sortido de pernas de cadeiras, cada senhora é única, como deveriam ser. Depois de revestidos, os assentos da coleção Rubens são frescos, higiênicos e totalmente rejuvenescidos. Há duas formas de dobrar os colchões, que criam uma versão compacta e uma versão assimétrica.

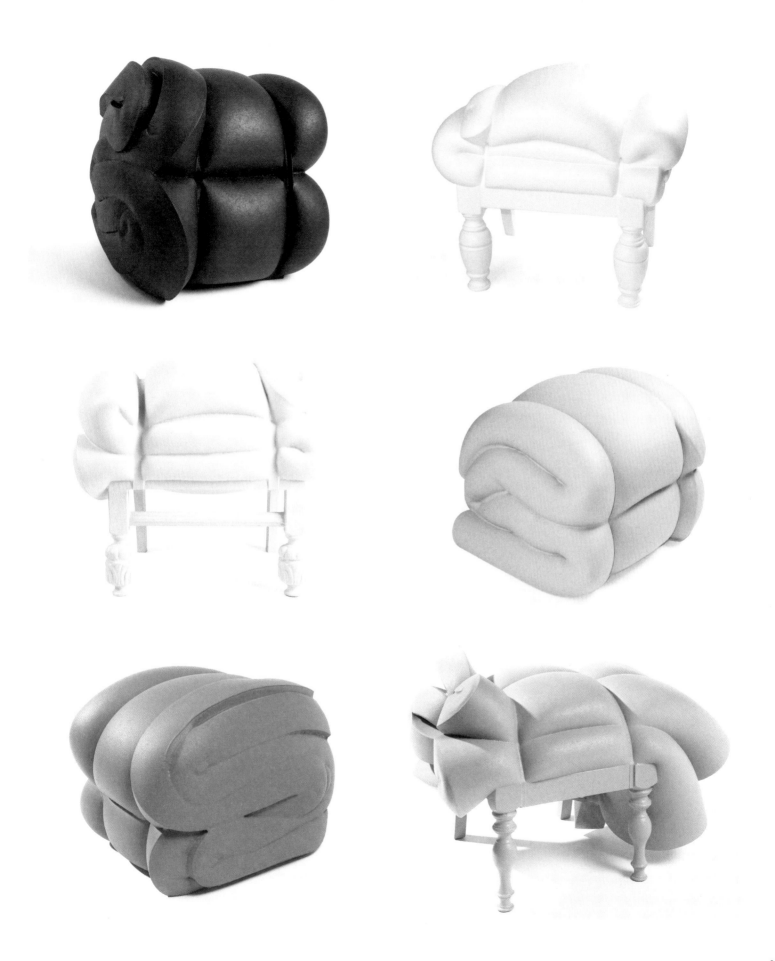

CAST COLLECTION

DESIGN FIRM
Reeves Design

DESIGNER
John Reeves

PHOTOGRAPHY
John Reeves & Vu Ha

CLIENT
REEVESdesign

The mighty Cast Aluminium Series One is the first REEVESdesign series to be made from solid recycled aluminum and FSC teak; there are certainly no synthetics here. Casting allows a simplicity of fabrication that ensures solid durability and also provides an opportunity to be more efficient during the production process, as any mistakes can be easily melted down and cast again. After formulating the initial concept sketch models were made and the designer worked with skilled carvers to make the wooden master to be used durings and casting. Carving the timber mold by hand is quite a juxtaposition with the rapid prototyping techniques that are being used in the West. Many cast products eventually find their way into a die-cast steel mold. However, Cast Aluminium Series One maintains the integrity of a hand-carved organic feel, enhancing the poetry, texture, and soul of the product.

FRA

La formidable collection Cast Aluminium Series One est la première de REEVESdesign réalisée en aluminium massif recyclé et en teck certifié FSC. Rien n'est synthétique ! Ce sont des produits solides qui résistent à l'usure du temps et aux intempéries. La fonte facilite la production et assure la solidité et la durabilité des pièces. Le processus de fabrication est efficace, et en cas d'erreur, la pièce non conforme peut être facilement refondue. Une fois le concept défini, des esquisses ont été réalisées. Le designer a ensuite travaillé avec des sculpteurs de haut niveau qui ont élaborés les matrices en bois des moules où le métal fondu est coulé. L'élaboration des moules en bois à la main n'a rien à voir avec les techniques de prototypage rapide utilisées en occident. La plupart des objets en fonte du marché sont produits dans des moules en acier. Les meubles de la série Cast, en revanche, ont l'esthétique de pièces sculptées à la main : elles ont l'aspect, la texture et l'âme des créations artisanales.

ESP

La potente Serie Uno de aluminio forjado es la primera serie de REEVESdesign fabricada con aluminio sólido reciclado y teca FSC; aquí no encontrará materiales sintéticos. Se trata de un producto resistente al paso del tiempo y los elementos. El forjado facilita la fabricación, de manera que el resultado es robusto y duradero. Además, el proceso de producción es más eficiente, ya que los productos defectuosos vuelven a fundirse y se forjan de nuevo. Después de formular el concepto se realizaron algunos modelos de prueba y el diseñador trabajó con ebanistas especializados para hacer la copia maestra de madera, que se usaría durante la fundición en arena. La talla artesana del molde de madera se yuxtapone a las rápidas técnicas que se aplican en los prototipos occidentales. Muchos productos forjados acaban en un molde de acero fundido. Sin embargo, la Serie Uno de aluminio forjado conserva el tacto orgánico de la talla artesana, realzando la poesía, la textura y el alma del producto.

POR

A poderosa Série Uno, de Alumínio Forjado, é a primeira série de REEVESdesign que se faz a partir de alumínio reciclado sólido e teca FSC; com certeza, aqui não há sintéticos. O forjamento permite uma simplicidade de fabricação que garante duração sólida e também proporciona uma oportunidade de maior eficiência durante o processo de produção, dado que se houver qualquer erro se poderá voltar a fundir e forjar de novo. Depois de formular o conceito inicial, se fizeram esboços e o designer trabalhou com gravadores especializados para fazer o molde de madeira, a ser utilizado durante a fundição em areia. Gravar o molde de madeira à mão é como uma justaposição com as rápidas técnicas prototípicas que se usam no Ocidente. Muitos produtos forjados acabam finalmente num molde de aço fundido. No entanto, a Série Uno de Alumínio Forjado mantém a integridade de um tato orgânico gravado à mão, realçando a poesia, a textura e a alma do produto.

SKETCH COLLECTION

DESIGN FIRM
Reeves Design

DESIGNER
John Reeves

PHOTOGRAPHY
John Reeves, Vu Ha, David Dinh

CLIENT
REEVESdesign

The surreal and organic form exploration was developed by loosely and impulsively drawing directly onto AutoCAD software using a computer tablet. Through this lucid engagement and direct communication, intuitively marking "cutting lines" and edges with the stroke of the stylus rather than the painstaking process of refining through nudging nodes and vectors, this form development was spontaneous and immediate. Each piece has a synthesis with another and all are similarly reminiscent of organic forms found in cave formations and nature. Each piece is signed and dated on the bottom by the designer, John Reeves. The designs in the Sketch collection are sand cast with care and great skill in 100 percent recycled aluminum. The solidness and weight of the pieces affirm their durability and longevity. Internally gilded drawer boxes enhance the specialness on the inside of these delicate, monolithic forms.

FRA
L'étude de formes organiques surréalistes est partie de dessins spontanés tracés directement dans AutoCAD à l'aide d'une tablette graphique. Ce mode d'interaction direct a permis de marquer de manière intuitive les lignes de coupe et les contours d'un coup de stylet au lieu de passer des heures à peaufiner des figures géométriques et des vecteurs : la conception a été spontanée et immédiate. Chaque pièce de la collection s'intègre harmonieusement aux autres. Les meubles évoquent les modelés karstiques ou les formes trouvées dans la nature. La signature du designer John Reeves et la date figurent au bas de chaque meuble de la série. Toutes les pièces de la collection Sketch sont coulées au sable avec le plus grand soin à partir d'aluminium recyclé. La solidité et le poids des meubles garantissent leur durabilité et leur longévité. L'intérieur des tiroirs a été doré, pour ajouter une touche d'originalité à ces formes monolithiques délicates.

ESP
La exploración de la forma surrealista y orgánica se desarrolló dibujando de forma libre e impulsiva en la aplicación AutoCAD de una tableta. Gracias a este compromiso lúcido y la comunicación directa, señalando intuitivamente las "líneas de corte" y los bordes con el trazo del lápiz óptico en lugar del proceso meticuloso de refinamiento mediante nodos y vectores, este desarrollo de la forma fue espontáneo e inmediato. Cada pieza se sintetiza con otra y todas ellas recuerdan a las formas orgánicas que se encuentran en las cavernas y la naturaleza. La base de cada pieza está firmada y datada por John Reeves. Los diseños de la colección Sketch están hechos de aluminio 100% reciclado, fundido en arena con gran destreza y cuidado. La dureza y el peso demuestran que son duraderos y longevos. El baño de oro del interior de los cajones realza lo extraordinario de estas formas delicadas y monolíticas.

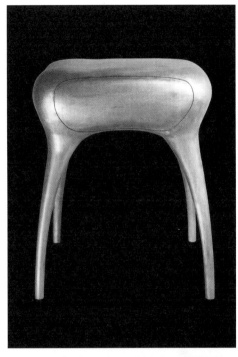

POR

A exploração da forma surrealista e orgânica desenvolveu-se ao desenhar livre e impulsivamente, diretamente num aplicativo AutoCAD de um tablet. Através deste compromisso lúcido e uma comunicação direta, marcando intuitivamente as "linhas de corte" e as bordas com o traço do lápis ótico, em vez do processo meticuloso de aperfeiçoar através de incômodos nós e vectores, este desenvolvimento da forma foi espontâneo e imediato. Cada peça sintetiza-se com outra e todas elas recordam, de modo semelhante, as formas orgânicas que se encontram em formações de grutas e natureza. Cada peça está assinada e datada em sua parte inferior pelo designer John Reeves. Os projetos da coleção Sketch são fundidos em areia, com muito cuidado e grande habilidade, em alumínio 100 % reciclado. A solidez e o peso das peças confirmam a sua durabilidade e longevidade. As gavetas chapeadas no interior realçam a especial qualidade destas formas delicadas e monolíticas.

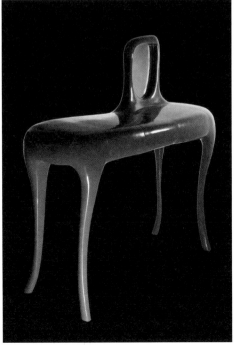

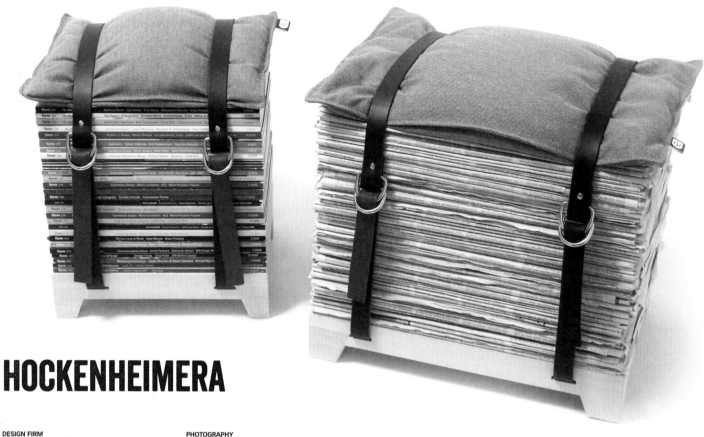

HOCKENHEIMERA

DESIGN FIRM
njustudio

DESIGNERS
Wolfgang Rößler, Kathrin Lang,
Tom Steinhöfer, Nina Wolf, Markus Mak

PHOTOGRAPHY
njustudio

CLIENT
njustudio

Daily newspapers and magazines no longer need to be kept on shelves or carelessly thrown away. Store them the njustudio way: amass, arrange, and take a seat! The Hockenheimer enables you to collect magazines and newspapers while simultaneously creating a sustainable and personalized piece of furniture. Start taking advantage of your subscriptions! The stand is made of birch and is smoothly manufactured by hand in a youth workshop near Coburg, Bavaria. The wood is waxed and given a brushed finish. Even the leather strapsare especially custom-made, with their buckles and rivets being attached by hand.

FRA
Fini les journaux et les magazines qui traînent partout ou encombrent les étagères. njustudio vous propose une autre méthode de rangement : rassembler, empiler et admirer ! Avec Hockenheimer, vous collectionnez journaux et magazines tout en créant un meuble à la fois durable et personnalisé. N'hésitez plus à vous abonner à vos revues préférées ! La base en bouleau est soigneusement fabriquée et poncée à la main dans un atelier de travail jeunesse près de Coburg en Bavière. Même les courroies en cuir fabriquées sur mesure avec leurs boucles et leurs rivets sont fixées à la main.

ESP
Ya no hace falta que guarde los periódicos y las revistas en las estanterías ni los tire de cualquier manera. Archívelos a la manera de njustudio: amontónelos, ordénelos ¡y siéntese tranquilamente! Gracias al Hockenheimer coleccionará revistas y periódicos al tiempo que crea un mueble sostenible y personalizado. ¡Aprovéchese de sus suscripciones! La base es de abedul y se fabrica con esmero en un taller de jóvenes situado en las inmediaciones de Coburg, Baviera. La madera está encerada y cepillada. Las correas de cuero también están personalizadas, con hebillas y remaches artesanales.

POR
Já não é necessário guardar jornais e revistas nas estantes ou jogá-los fora descuidadamente. Guarde-os ao modo de njustudio: agrupar, colocar e sentar-se! O Hockenheimer lhe permite colecionar revistas e jornais e simultaneamente criar um móvel sustentável e personalizado. Comece a tirar vantagem de suas assinaturas! A plataforma é feita de abeto e se fabrica com suavidade numa oficina de jovens, perto de Coburg, Baviera. A madeira se encera e recebe um acabamento escovado. Inclusive as correias de couro são personalizadas, com suas fivelas e rebites feitos à mão.

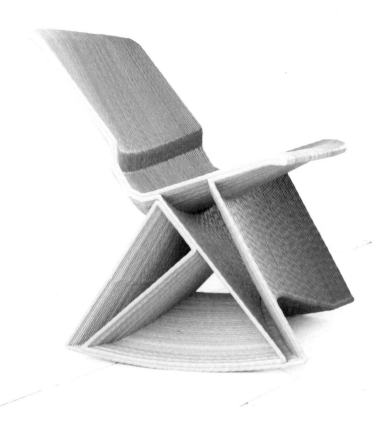

ENDLESS

DESIGNER
Dirk Vander Kooij

PHOTOGRAPHY
Dirk Vander Kooij

CLIENT
Dirk Vander Kooij

This is a collection of furniture with a unique building process. Layer by layer each piece is built from the ground up, using ground-up bits of refrigerators as a raw material.The traditional method for producing plastic chairs is injection molding. This process has the benefit of producing at a low cost, but it does need a large start up investment for the mold. This results in a highly inflexible process that offers no second chances, to the detriment of the design process.Craftsmanship is always the most flexible way of producing, but almost unaffordable nowadays. The process for Endless captures the flexibility of craftsmanship and combines it with the present possibilities of automation.

ESP
Esta colección de muebles tiene un proceso de fabricación único. Las piezas se construyen desde el suelo, una capa tras otra, usando fragmentos de frigoríficos como materia prima. El método tradicional para fabricar sillas de plástico es el moldeado por inyección. Este proceso tiene la ventaja de que es barato, pero se necesita una considerable inversión inicial para el molde. El resultado es un proceso muy inflexible, que no ofrece segundas oportunidades, en detrimento del proceso de diseño. La artesanía es mucho más flexible, pero actualmente es casi inasequible. El proceso de Eterno captura la flexibilidad de la artesanía y la combina con las posibilidades actuales de la automatización.

POR
Esta é uma coleção de móveis com um processo de construção único. Camada a camada, se constrói cada peça do chão para cima, usando pedaços pulverizados de geladeiras como matéria-prima. O método tradicional para produzir cadeiras de plástico é a moldagem por injeção. Este processo tem a vantagem de produzir a custo baixo, mas necessita de um grande investimento inicial para o molde. O resultado é um processo altamente inflexível, que não oferece segundas oportunidades, com prejuízo do processo de criação. O artesanato sempre é a forma mais flexível de produzir, mas hoje em dia é quase inacessível. O processo para Endless recolhe a flexibilidade do artesanato, combinando-a com as possibilidades atuais da automatização.

FRA
Voici une collection de meubles dont le mode de fabrication est unique en son genre. Chaque meuble est élaboré de la base au sommet en appliquant des couches successives d'une matière composée de débris de réfrigérateurs broyés. La méthode classique de fabrication d'une chaise en plastique est le moulage par injection. Si les coûts de production sont minimes, le moule représente un investissement de départ très élevé. Sans compter que ce système, extrêmement rigoureux, ne laisse aucune place à la créativité. À l'opposé, la méthode artisanale est celle qui permet la plus grande liberté, mais aujourd'hui son coût est prohibitif. Le mode de fabrication de la série Endless combine à la fois la souplesse d'un travail artisanal aux avantages de l'automatisation.

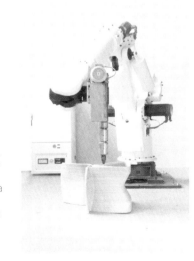

PROCESSED PAPER

DESIGN FIRM
Piadesign

PHOTOGRAPHY
Pia Wüstenberg

DESIGNER
Pia Wüstenberg

CLIENT
Utopia and Utility

This set of projects aims to exploit the properties of various paper components. Hollow paper legs are jointed to a plywood table top, which is hinged in the middle. The top can fold to transform from a coffee table with an embedded vase to a side table with a vase on top. Trestles are versatile objects that can be adapted for many different uses. Their main function is to hold weight, and thus the design aims to prove the structural properties of the paper components and construction. The aesthetic of the outcome is as much determined by the paper which is used to make the raw material as the way it is worked. All the paper used is collected from paper recycling bins or donated by printing companies.

FRA
Les meubles créés pour ce projet tirent parti des propriétés de différents éléments en papier. Des pieds de table creux en papier sont fixés à un plateau constitué de deux panneaux en contreplaqué unis par des charnières. Le plateau peut être plié en deux de manière à former une petite table basse, un des pieds servant de socle et l'autre de vase que l'on peut poser dessus. Les tréteaux sont des objets polyvalents que l'on peut adapter à toute sorte d'utilisations. Leur fonction principale étant de porter du poids, la forme ici vise à démontrer les propriétés structurelles des éléments en papier et de l'armature. L'esthétique de l'ensemble dépend à la fois du papier utilisé comme matière première et de la façon dont il est travaillé. Il est à noter que le papier employé pour fabriquer les meubles est collecté dans les conteneurs de recyclage ou donné par des imprimeries.

ESP
Este conjunto de proyectos trata de explotar las propiedades de las partes de papel. Así, las patas huecas están unidas a la superficie de madera contrachapada de la mesa, que dispone de un juego de bisagras en el medio, de manera que puede doblarse para transformarse de una mesita de café con un jarrón incrustado a una mesa auxiliar con un jarrón encima. Los caballetes son objetos versátiles que se adaptan a usos muy diversos. Su función más importante es la de carga, de manera que el diseño aspira a demostrar las propiedades estructurales de las partes de papel y la construcción. La materia prima, así como la forma en la que esta se trabaja, determinan la estética del resultado. Todo el papel se obtiene en papeleras de reciclaje de papel o lo donan empresas de reprografía.

POR
Este conjunto de projetos pretende explorar as propriedades de vários componentes do papel. Pernas vazias de papel se unem a uma superfície de mesa compensada, que tem dobradiças no meio. A parte superior pode ser dobrada para se transformar a partir de uma mesa de café com um jarro incrustado em uma mesa auxiliar com um jarro em cima. Os cavaletes são objetos versáteis que se podem adaptar a muitos usos diferentes. Sua função principal é suportar peso, e deste modo o projeto aspira experimentar as propriedades estruturais dos componentes do papel e a construção. A estética do resultado é determinada tanto pelo papel que se usa como matéria-prima como pela forma em que se trabalha. Todo o papel que se usa é recolhido de indústrias de reciclagem de papel ou é doado por empresas gráficas.

PAPERPULP

DESIGN FIRM
Studio Debbie Wijskamp

DESIGNER
Debbie Wijskamp

PHOTOGRAPHY
Debbie Wijskamp

Inspired by different cultures that make their homes with materials found in their surroundings, Debbie Wijskamp wanted to make her own building material. Experimenting with reusing waste paper resulted in a material with its own characteristic appearance and structure. This material is also very versatile and has many possible applications. The Paperpulp cabinets are entirely made from this "new old" material, constructed from various oblong boards stacked upon one another. Some parts have drawers, while others are left open to function as shelves. In contrast with the cabinets, the Paperpulp vessels are very fragile decorative objects. The colors of the vessels depend on the ink of the newspapers from which they are made, making every single bowl unique.

FRA

S'inspirant des multiples cultures où l'on fabrique sa maison avec les éléments que l'on trouve à sa portée, Debbie Wijskamp a décidé de créer son propre matériau de construction. Après de nombreux essais avec du papier de récupération, elle a réussi à mettre au point un matériau doté de caractéristiques propres tant du point de vue de son aspect que de sa structure. Ce matériau est par ailleurs polyvalent, puisqu'il peut être exploité de diverses façons. Les meubles de rangement sont entièrement fabriqués dans cette matière « neuve-vieille », à partir de lattes juxtaposées. Certains meubles sont équipés de tiroirs, d'autres sont de simples structures ouvertes servant d'étagères. Contrairement aux meubles, les vases Paperpulp sont des objets de décoration très fragiles. La couleur de ces vases est fonction de l'encre utilisée sur les pages des journaux recyclés, ce qui explique qu'il n'y en ait pas deux pareils.

ESP

Inspirándose en las culturas que construyen sus casas con los materiales que encuentran en los alrededores, Debbie Wijskamp quería un material de construcción propio. Los experimentos con papel reciclado dieron como resultado un material con apariencia y estructura características, que además era muy versátil y ofrecía muchas aplicaciones. Los armarios de Pulpa de papel están completamente hechos de este material "nuevo viejo", con diversas tablas rectangulares apiladas una encima de otra. Algunas partes tienen cajones, mientras que otras han quedado abiertas y hacen las veces de estanterías. Al contrario que los armarios, los jarrones de Pulpa de papel son objetos decorativos sumamente frágiles. Sus colores dependen de la tinta de los periódicos con los que se fabrican, de manera que cada vasija es única.

POR

Inspirada em diferentes culturas que constroem seus lares com materiais encontrados nos arredores, Debbie Wijskamp queria fazer seu próprio material de construção. A experiência de reutilizar papel descartado deu como resultado um material com aparência e estrutura próprias. Este material também é muito versátil e tem muitas aplicações possiveis. Os armários Polpa de papel são feitos totalmente a partir deste material "novo velho", construídos de várias tabelas retangulares empilhadas umas em cima das outras. Algumas partes têm gavetas, enquanto outras foram deixadas abertas para servir como estantes. Em contraste com os armários, os jarros Polpa de papel são objetos decorativos muito frágeis. As cores dos jarros dependem da tinta dos jornais de que são feitos, tornando cada tigela em única.

DVELAS

DESIGN FIRM
DVELAS

DESIGNER
Enrique Kahle

PHOTOGRAPHY
L. Ambrós, L. Prieto, J. Moreno

The DVELAS design team endeavors to salvage used sails and transform them into exclusive contemporary designs. The initiative emerged as a creative reaction aimed at harnessing the vast amount of material discarded from sailing ships by finding new design methods and inspiration in their aesthetics, materials, techniques, and forms.
The team is organized as a working group that explores the fusion of two different activities, namelysail making and design, decontextualizing both their materials and techniques and applying them to the field of furniture design.

FRA

L'équipe de concepteurs de la gamme DVELAS se consacre à la récupération de voiles qu'elle transforme en meubles hyper design. L'initiative a vu le jour pour tenter d'exploiter de manière créative l'énorme quantité de toile mise au rebut par les voiliers : il fallait trouver de nouvelles méthodes de conception et s'inspirer de leur esthétique particulière, ainsi que de leurs matières, techniques et formes. L'équipe fonctionne comme un groupe de travail dont l'objectif est de fusionner deux activités différentes, à savoir la fabrication de voiles et le design, tout en décontextualisant les matériaux et les techniques pour les appliquer à la conception de meubles.

ESP

El equipo de diseño DVELAS trata de reciclar velas y transformarlas en exclusivos diseños contemporáneos. La iniciativa surgió como una reacción creativa frente a las grandes cantidades de materiales que desechan los barcos, encontrando nuevos métodos de diseño e inspiración en la estética, los materiales, las técnicas y las formas de estos. El equipo se organiza a la manera de un grupo de trabajo que explora la fusión de dos actividades diferentes, concretamente la confección de velas y el diseño, descontextualizando tanto los materiales como las técnicas y aplicándolos al campo del diseño de muebles.

POR

A equipe de projeto DVELAS trata de salvar velas usadas e transformá-las em criações exclusivas contemporâneas. A iniciativa surgiu como uma reação criativa cujo objetivo era usar a enorme quantidade de material rejeitado dos barcos de navegação, encontrando novos métodos de concepção e inspiração em sua estética, seus materiais, técnicas e formas. A equipe está organizada como grupo de trabalho que explora a fusão de duas atividades diferentes, especificamente a confecção de velas e o design, descontextualizando tanto seus materiais como suas técnicas e aplicando os mesmos ao campo do design de móveis.

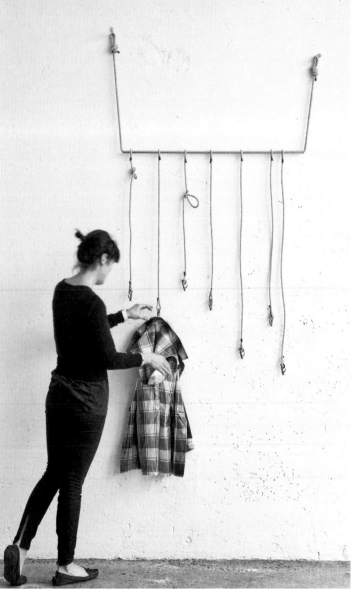

NOT SO FRAGILE

DESIGN FIRM
UXUS

PHOTOGRAPHY
Dim Balsem

Not So Fragile is a one-of-a-kind, repurposed furniture collection composed in neon-orange packing tape, taking on a new life and shedding expected perceptions to become evocative furniture elements. This is furniture for the postmaterialist, a collection that is at once unique, sustainable, and iconic.

FRA
Not So Fragile est une collection unique en son genre d'objets rénovés avec du ruban d'emballage orange fluo qui donne un coup de jeune aux meubles et les transforme en éléments de décoration. Cette collection, qui s'adresse aux postmatérialistes, propose des meubles originaux, durables et emblématiques.

ESP
No tan frágil es una colección de muebles única, replanteada y elaborada con cinta adhesiva naranja neón en la que los muebles cobran una nueva vida, despojándose de ideas preconcebidas y haciéndose evocadores. Son muebles para posmaterialistas, una colección única, sostenible e icónica al mismo tiempo.

POR
Não tão frágil é uma coleção de móveis única, repensada, elaborada com fita de embalagem laranja néon, que ganha uma nova vida e se despoja de percepções esperadas para se tornarem evocativos elementos de móveis. Estes móveis destinam-se aos pós-materialistas, uma coleção que é simultaneamente única, sustentável e iconográfica.

RD LEGS CHAIR

DESIGN FIRM
Cohda Design

DESIGNER
Richard Liddle

PHOTOGRAPHY
Cohda Design

RD (Roughly Drawn) Legs Chairs are hand woven in 100 percent recycled plastic. Building on the early experimental plastic processes developed by Richard Liddle at Cohda, the design uses no glues or additional fixings in its production. All that's added is heat and skill. This design has been widely recognized as one of the major iconic eco products of the first decade of the twenty-first century and was shortlisted in the Innovation category in the Classic Design Awards at London's Victoria and Albert Museum.The chairs are hand made in the UK from 100 percent recycled, domestic HDPE (High Density Polyethylene) plastic waste, consisting of milk bottles, detergent bottles, and food trays.

FRA

Le revêtement des chaises RD Legs est tissé à la main dans du plastique 100 % recyclé. Basé sur les premiers procédés de fabrication expérimentale du plastique de Richard Liddle chez Cohda, nul besoin de colle ni d'élément de fixation pour produire ce modèle. Il suffit d'un peu de chaleur et d'un certain savoir-faire. Cette chaise a été reconnue dans le monde entier comme un des produits écologiques phares de la première décennie du XXIe siècle, et a participé au concours « Classic Design Awards », dans la catégorie Innovation du Victoria and Albert Museum de Londres. Les chaises sont faites à la main au Royaume-Uni à partir de plastique 100 % recyclé, soit des déchets plastiques domestiques PEHD (polyéthylène haute densité) – bouteilles de lait, bidons de détergents et barquettes alimentaires.

ESP

Las sillas de patas TD (toscamente dibujadas) están tejidas a mano con plástico 100 % reciclado. Basándose en los primeros procesos experimentales con plástico que desarrollara Richard Liddle en Cohda, la fabricación del diseño no emplea colas ni accesorios adicionales. Lo único que se añade es afecto y destreza. Este diseño ha sido ampliamente reconocido como una de las creaciones ecológicas icónicas más destacadas de la primera década del siglo XXI y fue preseleccionado en la categoría de Innovación para los Premios de Diseño Clásico del Museo de Victoria y Alberto de Londres. Las sillas se fabrican a mano en el Reino Unido con residuos de plástico casero PEAD (polietileno de alta densidad) 100 % reciclados, consistentes en botellas de leche y detergente y bandejas de comida.

POR

As cadeiras de pernas TD (toscamente desenhadas) são tecidas a mão, em plástico 100 % reciclado. Construindo sobre os primeiros processos experimentais com plástico, desenvolvidos por Richard Liddle em Cohda, o projeto não usa colas ou fixações adicionadas em sua produção. Tudo o que se adiciona é calor e habilidade. Este design foi reconhecido amplamente como um dos principais produtos iconográficos eco da primeira década do século vinte e um, e foi pré-selecionado na categoria de Inovação nos Prêmios de Design Clássico no Museu de Vitória e Alberto, Londres. As cadeiras são feitas a mão no Reino Unido a partir de resíduos 100 % reciclados de plástico caseiro PEAD (polietileno de alta densidade), que consistem em garrafas de leite, garrafas de detergente e bandejas de comida.

PANDORA

DESIGNER
Sander Mulder

PHOTOGRAPHY
Manuel Milde & Sander Mulder

Known the world over for its indestructible appearance and boxy look, the shipping container is one of the best-known industrial archetypes. This modular storage system is inspired by the wonderful color mosaics that sprout to life in every harbor and container terminal the world over. The individual pieces can be stacked and rotated around in endless combinations to create your personal container terminal for all domestic storage uses.

FRA
Connu dans le monde entier pour son aspect de coffre indestructible, le conteneur est un des archétypes industriels les plus répandus. Ce système de rangement modulaire trouve son inspiration dans les magnifiques mosaïques colorées que l'on retrouve dans tous les ports et terminaux de conteneurs du globe. On peut empiler les modules et les placer horizontalement ou verticalement pour créer de multiples combinaisons et produire son propre terminal de conteneurs pour ranger toutes ses affaires.

POR
Conhecidos em todo o mundo por sua aparência indestrutível e sua imagem quadrada, o contêiner de envios é um dos arquétipos industriais mais conhecidos. Este sistema de estocagem modular inspira-se nos maravilhosos mosaicos de cores que ganham vida em cada porto e em cada terminal de contêineres em todo o mundo. As peças individuais podem ser empilhadas e girar em infindáveis combinações para criar o seu próprio terminal pessoal de contêineres para todo o tipo de usos de estocagem caseira.

ESP
Los contenedores, cuya imagen cuadrada y apariencia indestructible son famosas en todo el mundo, constituyen uno de los arquetipos industriales más conocidos. Este sistema de almacenaje modular se inspira en los hermosos mosaicos de colores que cobran vida en todos los puertos y terminales de contenedores del mundo. Los componentes individuales pueden apilarse y darse la vuelta en infinitas combinaciones, creando terminales personalizadas para todo tipo de almacenaje casero.

STUMP SERIES

DESIGN FIRM
Ubico Studio

DESIGNERS
Ori Ben-Zvi & Ellia Nattel

The Stump series started in the industrial garbage cans located near Ubico Studio, in the form of the small pieces of hardwood thrown away in abundant quantities from carpentry workshops in the area. Through developing the series it became clear that cost reduction and social involvement could be achieved by passing some of the production to a factory that rehabilitates people with disabilities.

The main aim of the Stump series was to generate objects based on industrial waste that incorporate a social value and visually embody their recycled nature. The process started with a study of potential raw materials and ended up focusing on relatively small pieces of hardwood thrown away in large quantities by the carpentry industry.

FRA
La série Stump a démarré à partir de chutes de bois de feuillus que l'on trouvait en grande quantité dans les poubelles industrielles situées près des studios, et où les nombreuses menuiseries et ateliers du quartier jetaient leurs déchets.
À mesure que nous développions la série, il nous semblait de plus en plus évident que pour réduire nos coûts tout en étant utiles à la société, nous devions confier une partie de la production à une usine employant du personnel handicapé.
L'objectif de la série Stump était de créer des objets à partir de déchets industriels qui puissent servir une cause sociale sans pour autant cacher leur nature recyclée. Le projet a commencé par l'étude de matériaux bruts potentiels pour choisir finalement les chutes de bois de feuillus de taille relativement réduite rejetées en grande quantité par les menuiseries industrielles.

ESP
La serie Stump empezó en los cubos de basura industriales situados en los alrededores de Ubico Studio, en forma de los trocitos de madera dura que tiraban en grandes cantidades los talleres de carpintería del barrio. A medida que desarrollaban la serie, los diseñadores observaron que si desplazaban una parte de la producción a una fábrica en la que se rehabilitaban personas discapacitadas reducirían los costes y se implicarían socialmente.
El mayor objetivo de la serie Stump era crear objetos basados en residuos industriales que tuvieran valor social y encarnasen visualmente esta naturaleza reciclada. El proceso comenzó con un estudio de la materia prima en potencia y acabó concentrándose en los trozos de madera dura relativamente pequeños que la industria carpintera desechaba en grandes cantidades.

POR
A série Stump começou nas latas de lixo industriais situadas perto da Localizo Studio, em forma de tocos de madeira dura descartados em quantidades abundantes pelas oficinas de carpintaria da zona. Ao desenvolver a série, se viu que se poderia conseguir uma redução dos custos e obter maior envolvimento social ao passar parte da produção a uma fábrica que reabilita pessoas deficientes.
O objetivo principal da série Stump era gerar objetos baseados em resíduos industriais que incorporassem valor social e que encarnassem visualmente sua natureza reciclada. O processo começou com um estudo da matéria-prima potencial e acabou centrando-se em pedaços de madeira dura, relativamente pequenos, descartados em grandes quantidades pela indústria de carpintaria.

BLOCKSHELF

DESIGNER
Amy Hunting

PHOTOGRAPHY
Amy Hunting

CLIENT
Green Furniture Sweden

The wood is collected from a local timber importer's waste bin in London and consists of over twenty sorts of untreated wood. This is the first result of the designer's experiments with rope and wood. Using the beautiful wood-waste mix that comes out of the massive wooden-flooring industry, this shelf says "recycled" with pride! Each shelf is unique and can easily be reconfigured by the user. It can be hung on a wall or from the ceiling, where it can also function as a thin room divider.

FRA
Le principe de cette collection paraît évident : que peut-on faire avec des planches en bois et des cordes en coton ? Les étagères sont assemblées à l'aide de nœuds marins que l'on peut défaire très facilement en tirant simplement sur la corde. Quant aux planches, elles sont fabriquées dans du bois de récupération provenant du conteneur de déchets d'un importateur londonien de bois. Il s'agit de vingt variétés de bois non traité. Nous voyons ici le résultat des premières expériences d'Amy Hunting associant bois et corde.

ESP
La materia prima (más de veinte clases distintas de madera no tratada) se obtiene en el cubo de basura de una empresa londinense de importación de madera. Este es el primer resultado de los experimentos de la diseñadora con cuerdas y madera. Gracias a la hermosa combinación de residuos y madera de la boyante industria del parqué, ¡esta estantería dice "reciclada" con orgullo! Cada estantería es única y puede reconfigurarse fácilmente al gusto del usuario. Puede colgarse de las paredes o del techo, donde también hace las veces de fina separación de habitaciones.

POR
A madeira é recolhida dos descartes de um importador local de madeira em Londres e consiste em mais de vinte tipos de madeira sem tratamento. Este é o primeiro resultado das experiências da designer com cordas e madeira. Usando a preciosa mistura de resíduos e madeira que surge da sólida indústria de parquets, esta estante se diz "reciclada" com orgulho! Cada estante é única e pode ser reconfigurada facilmente pelo usuário. Pode ser pendurada numa parede ou no teto, onde também pode funcionar como uma fina divisória para o quarto.

THE PATCHWORK COLLECTION

DESIGNER
Amy Hunting

PHOTOGRAPHY
Amy Hunting

CLIENT
Green Furniture Swede

The book box has built-in book stands, allowing you to place different-sized books randomly in the box without them falling over. The boxes can be stacked on top of each other or hung on a wall. You can flip the box and use it on its side, with the legs then becoming additional shelves. Like the chair and the lamps in the same collection, the book box is made entirely out of wood waste from factories in Denmark, with no screws, bolts, or anything else. The lamps were cut out of a large, solid block of wood, made up of small offcuts. The pendant lamps were then cut out of the block until twelve lamps revealed themselves and all the wood had been cut out. They are made entirely out of wood and require no fitting. They can be hung on any bare lamp bulb through the top of the lamp. The twelve lamps can be stacked inside each other for easy transport or stacked on top of each other.

FRA
Ce casier bibliothèque intègre des appuis-livres qui permettent de ranger au hasard des volumes de différentes tailles sans qu'ils tombent. On peut empiler plusieurs casiers ou les fixer au mur. Il est également possible de poser le casier sur le côté, les pieds servant alors d'étagères supplémentaires. Le casier, tout comme la chaise et les abats-jours de la collection, sont entièrement fabriqués à partir de chutes provenant d'usines danoises. Ils n'utilisent ni vis, ni boulon, ni aucun autre système de fixation. Les abats-jours ont été découpés dans un gros bloc de bois constitué à partir de chutes. Douze abats-jours ont pu être taillés dans le même bloc. Ils sont entièrement faits en bois. Il suffit d'accrocher l'abat-jour sur une ampoule nue suspendue au plafond pour disposer d'un magnifique lustre. Les abats-jours peuvent être emboîtés les uns dans les autres pour faciliter leur transport ou être empilés l'un sur l'autre.

Las cajas de libros cuentan con soportes integrados que le permiten colocar libros de diferentes tamaños al azar sin que se caigan. Pueden apilarse una encima de otra o colgarse de las paredes. Si les da vuelta para usarlas de lado las patas se convierten en estanterías adicionales. Al igual que la silla y las lámparas de la misma colección, las cajas de libros están completamente hechas de residuos de madera provenientes de fábricas danesas y no utilizan tornillos, pernos ni nada. Las lámparas están talladas en un bloque de madera grande y fuerte y se componen de trocitos sobrantes. A continuación se tallaron las lámparas colgantes hasta que aparecieron doce lámparas y se hubo cortado toda la madera. Están completamente hechas de madera y no requieren accesorios. Pueden colgarse en cualquier bombilla desnuda a través de la parte superior de la pantalla. Las doce lámparas pueden guardarse una dentro de otra para transportarlas fácilmente o apilarse una encima de otra.

POR

A caixa de livros tem suportes integrados para livros, permitindo-lhe colocar na caixa, ao acaso, livros de diferentes tamanhos sem que eles caiam uns em cima dos outros. As caixas podem ser empilhadas umas em cima das outras ou podem ser penduradas numa parede. Pode-se tombar a caixa e usar a mesma de lado, com as pernas convertendo-se em estantes adicionais. Assim como a cadeira e os lustres da mesma coleção, a caixa de livros é feita, totalmente, de resíduos de madeira provenientes de fábricas na Dinamarca, sem parafusos, pinos nem nada mais. Os lustres foram cortados de um bloco sólido e grande de madeira, feito de pequenos restos. Depois, os lustres suspensos foram cortados do bloco até que doze lâmpadas ficaram a descoberto até terminar de cortar toda a madeira. Estão totalmente feitos de madeira e não requerem ajustes. Podem ser pendurados em qualquer lâmpada nua através da parte superior da lâmpada. Os doze lustres podem ser empilhados um dentro do outro para facilitar o transporte ou empilhados um em cima do outro.

02
56-101

FRA

MATÉRIAUX NATURELS

Si l'on compare les matières synthétiques produites par l'homme, comme le plastique, aux matériaux naturels, il est clair que la fabrication d'objets à partir de ces derniers est plus écologique. Ils consomment moins de ressources et requièrent moins de traitements que les produits synthétiques : leur usage limite la pollution de l'environnement et la production de CO2, dangereux pour la santé. Dans le monde du design de mobilier, l'utilisation de matériaux naturels est d'autant plus logique que presque tout le monde vit entourés de meubles, que ce soit à la maison ou à l'extérieur, et que cela nous permet de profiter davantage de la nature , tout en protégeant l'environnement.

POR

MATERIAIS NATURAIS

Quando se trata de produzir, os materiais naturais são muito melhores para o meio ambiente em comparação com os materiais sintéticos e artificiais como o plástico. Consomem menos recursos, não requerem os recursos ou processos que são necessários para fabricar materiais artificiais e, além disso, usar materiais naturais reduz a contaminação ambiental e as perigosas emissões de carbono à atmosfera. Para o mundo do design, produzir móveis a partir de materiais naturais tem ainda mais sentido, não só porque quase todo o mundo usa móveis em casa, em lugares públicos e, inclusive, em espaços exteriores, mas também porque usar materiais naturais para os móveis nos permite usufruir do mundo natural à nossa volta e, simultaneamente, melhorar e proteger o meio ambiente.

ESP

MATERIALES NATURALES

En el ámbito de la fabricación, los materiales naturales son mucho mejores para el medioambiente que los materiales sintéticos y artificiales como el plástico; consumen menos recursos y como no requieren los mismos recursos ni procesos que los materiales artificiales disminuyen la contaminación y las peligrosas emisiones de carbono a la atmósfera. En el mundo del diseño, la creación de muebles con materiales naturales tiene todavía más sentido, no solo porque se usan muebles en casi todas las casas, lugares públicos e incluso espacios exteriores, sino también porque gracias a los muebles de materiales naturales disfrutamos del mundo que nos rodea y al mismo tiempo mejoramos y protegemos el medioambiente.

NATURAL MATERIALS

Compared with synthetic and manmade materials such as plastic, when it comes to manufacturing natural materials are much better for the environment. They consume fewer resources, and because they also do not require the resources or processes that are necessary to make manmade materials, using natural materials reduces environmental pollution and dangerous carbon emissions into the atmosphere. For the design world, producing furniture from natural materials makes even more sense, not just because almost everyone uses furniture at home, in public places, and even outside spaces, but also because using natural materials for furniture allows us to enjoy the natural world around us and, at the same, to improve and protect the environment.

UPSIDE DOWN LOUNGE

DESIGN FIRM
Studio Floris Wubben

DESIGNER
Floris Wubben

PHOTOGRAPHY
Floris Wubben

CRAFTSMANSHIP
Bauke Fokkema

CLIENT
Anthropologie, New York

Dutch designer Floris Wubben was inspired by nature to create this comfortable, naturally grown chair. Wubben made this original piece of furniture using a willow tree. This type of tree usually has many narrow and elastic branches, which seem to grow from a kind of "head". Wubben forced the tree's branches to grow into four legs. After the trunk was cut off and inverted this amazing project was completed by carving a seat into the wood. This project was jointly produced with the artist Bauke Fokkema.

FRA
La créatrice hollandaise Floris Wubben s'est inspirée de la nature pour concevoir cette chaise confortable qui a l'air d'avoir poussé toute seule. Elle a fabriqué ce meuble original à partir du tronc d'un saule. Cette variété d'arbre est le plus souvent dotée de nombreuses branches minces et souples qui tombent vers le sol comme une ample chevelure. Floris Wubben a forcé la pousse des branches de manière à former quatre pieds. L'arbre a ensuite été scié et la cime posée à l'envers. Puis, la chaise a été sculptée dans le bois. Ce projet a été réalisé conjointement avec l'artiste Bauke Fokkema.

ESP
El diseñador holandés Floris Wubben se inspiró en la naturaleza para crear esta confortable silla cultivada con medios naturales. Wubben fabricó esta original pieza con un sauce. Estos árboles suelen tener abundantes ramas estrechas y elásticas que aparentemente brotan de una especie de "cabeza"; Wubben las dobló de manera que creciesen en forma de cuatro patas, cortó el tronco, le dio la vuelta y remató este increíble proyecto tallando un asiento en la madera. Se trata de una producción conjunta con el artista Bauke Fokkema.

POR
O Designer holandês Floris Wubbem se inspirou na natureza para criar esta cadeira cômoda, cheia naturalmente. Wubbem fez este móvel original usando um salgueiro. Este tipo de árvore normalmente tem muitos ramos estreitos e elásticos, que parecem crescer a partir de um tipo de "cabeça". Wubbem forçou que os ramos da árvore crescessem em quatro pernas. Depois de cortar o tronco e inverter o mesmo, este incrível projeto se completou o talhar um assento na madeira. Este projeto foi produzido em conjunto com o artista Bauke Fokkema.

TAMED NATURE STOOL

DESIGNER
Juozas Urbonavic ius

PHOTOGRAPHY
Juozas Urbonavic ius & Vaigirdas Kofy

In this work wild nature is subjected to function, though at the same time the uniqueness and originality of the primary material is preserved and emphasized. It is possible to take adualistic view of this stool. In it one can either see nature, tamed to work for functionality, or alternatively the liberated spirit of functional objects.The stool is made from solid pine and plum-tree branches. Inexpensive materials—offcuts and dry, trimmed branches—were used to produce the object. The top of the stool is covered with linseed oil and for the joints only glue was used. The defining look of this stool is raw branches. In spite of its improvised look, the stool is very stable and comfortable.

FRA

Ici, la nature sauvage est assujettie à la fonction, bien que l'originalité de la matière première soit conservée et mise en valeur. En fait, on peut voir ce tabouret de deux façons : soit comme le résultat de la nature domestiquée pour servir une fonction donnée, soit comme l'esprit naturel des objets fonctionnels. Le tabouret est fabriqué dans du pin et des branches de prunier : ce sont des matériaux bon marché — chutes de bois et branches taillées. L'assise du tabouret a été traitée à l'huile de lin. Les pieds ont été fixés avec de la colle. Ce qui attire l'attention sur ce tabouret est résolument son piètement en branches brutes. En dépit de son aspect improvisé, le tabouret est particulièrement stable et confortable.

ESP

En esta obra, la naturaleza salvaje se somete a la función, aunque al mismo tiempo se conserva y se subraya el carácter original y único de la materia prima. Es posible contemplarla desde una perspectiva dualista. En el taburete se observa la naturaleza, doblegada al servicio de la función, así como el espíritu liberado de los objetos funcionales. Está hecho de pino robusto y ramas de ciruelo, con materiales económicos, como trozos de madera y ramas podadas secas. La superficie tiene una capa de aceite de linaza y en las juntas solo se ha usado cola. El elemento más característico son las ramas en bruto. Aunque parece improvisado, se trata de taburete muy estable y cómodo.

POR

Nesta obra, a natureza selvagem submete-se à função, embora simultaneamente se conserva e se enfatiza a singularidade e originalidade da matéria primária. É possível captar uma perspectiva dualista deste tamborete. Nele, se pode ver a natureza, domada para trabalhar para a funcionalidade ou, alternativamente, o espírito libertador de objetos funcionais. O tamborete é feito de pinheiro sólido e ramos de ameixeira. Foram usados materiais econômicos —pedaços de madeira e ramos secos e podados— para produzir o objeto. A superfície do tamborete está recoberta de óleo de linhaça e para as juntas só se utilizou cola. A aparência que define este tamborete é a dos ramos sem tratamento. Apesar de sua aparência improvisada, o tamborete é muito estável e cômodo.

MAGISTRAL CABINET

DESIGNER
Sebastian Errazuriz

PHOTOGRAPHY
Sebastian Errazuriz

Walking the fine line between art and design, this sculptural cabinet continues the artist's investigation into the boundaries between functionality and symbolism. A protective layer made up of eighty thousand bamboo skewers covers the cabinet like protective armor, safely holding personal belongings in its interior. A set of concealed doors slides open to reveal its inner mechanisms and many compartments. The construction process required a total of six weeks for a team of twelve woodworkers to hammer each skewer individually into the previously carved wooden structure.

ESP

A caballo entre el arte y el diseño, este armario escultórico, ahonda en la investigación del artista en los límites entre lo funcional y lo simbólico. Una capa de ochenta mil pinchos de bambú recubre el armario a la manera de una armadura protectora, guardando celosamente los efectos personales que alberga. Al abrirse un conjunto de puertas corredizas ocultas se descubren sus mecanismos internos y sus muchos compartimientos. El proceso de fabricación requirió de seis semanas para que un equipo de doce carpinteros clavase cada uno de los pinchos en la estructura de madera tallada de antemano.

FRA

Cette armoire sculpturale, à la croisée entre l'art et le design, et dont le travail porte sur l'étude de la frontière séparant le fonctionnel du symbolisme. Une enveloppe protectrice composée de quatre-vingt mille baguettes de bambou recouvre l'armoire, telle une carapace, pour protéger les objets personnels rangés à l'intérieur. Un jeu de portes coulissantes révèle ses mécanismes internes et ses multiples compartiments. Le processus de fabrication minutieux nécessite beaucoup de main d'œuvre : il faut six semaines à une équipe de douze menuisiers pour enfoncer chacune des baguettes dans les trous préalablement percés dans la structure.

POR

Caminhando na estreita linha entre arte e design, este escultural armário, continua a pesquisa do artista nos limites entre funcionalidade e simbolismo. Uma camada protetora feita de oitenta mil pontas de bambu cobre o armário como uma armadura protetora, guardando com segurança os pertences pessoais em seu interior. Um conjunto de portas escondidas deslizam para se abrirem e revelar seus mecanismos internos e muitos compartimentos. O obsessivo processo de construção mediante um intenso trabalho exigiu um total de seis semanas para que uma equipe de doze carpinteiros cravasse cada ponta individualmente na estrutura de madeira previamente talhada.

BAMBOO CELL NO.2

DESIGNER
Fanson Meng

PHOTOGRAPHY
Fanson Meng

The form and texture of bamboo feature on the surface of the seat, with the slices of hollow bamboo stalks used to make the seat allowing the user to appreciate the inner fiber of bamboo while sitting. The use of modern polyester resin as a molding material makes the bamboo stand out, and differentiates this bench from furniture made with traditional crafting processes. The contrast of materials allows bamboo to be viewed from a different perspective and also strengthens the surface of the seat.

FRA

La surface de l'assise reflète la forme et la texture des tiges. La personne qui s'assoit sur le banc peut ainsi admirer les fibres de leur corps creux tout en se reposant. L'emploi de résine polyester pour le moulage fait ressortir le bambou et donne au banc un aspect bien différent de celui des meubles artisanaux fabriqués habituellement dans ce matériau. Le contraste des matières met en lumière la face cachée du bambou tout en renforçant la solidité de l'assise.

ESP

En la superficie del asiento se observan la forma y la textura del bambú mediante cañas huecas con las que el usuario aprecia las fibras interiores cuando se sienta. El uso de la resina de poliéster moderna en el modelado hace que destaque el bambú y distingue este banco de otros muebles fabricados mediante procesos de tallado tradicionales. Gracias al contraste de materiales el bambú se contempla desde perspectivas diferentes y refuerza la superficie del asiento.

POR

A forma e textura do bambu caracterizam a superfície do assento, com tiras de canas de bambu vazias usadas para fazer o assento e que permitem ao usuário apreciar as fibras interiores do bambu enquanto estiver sentado. A composição das canas tem a aparência de células de plantas vistas sob a lente de um microscópio. O uso de resina moderna de poliéster como material de modelagem destaca o bambu, e diferencia este banco de outros móveis feitos com processos de entalhes tradicionais. O contraste de materiais permite que o bambu seja visto de perspectivas diversas e também reforça a superfície do assento.

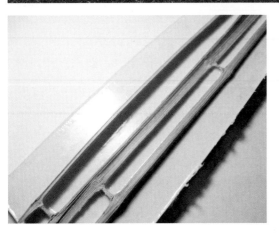

BAMBOO CELL

DESIGNER
Fanson Meng

PHOTOGRAPHY
Fanson Meng

Bamboo Cell is a stool with a polyester-resin seat, into which bamboo legs have been set along with a number of bamboo rings. The design of the seat is suggestive of the densely packed cells of a piece of bamboo, which can be clearly seen when the plant is viewed under a microscope. The hollowness of the legs manifests itself in the seat, with this feature also making the stool easy to grab and pick up. The bamboo-piece pattern enhances the strength of the molded resin. The stool could easily be mass-produced, though each piece would still be unique.

FRA
Bamboo Cell est un tabouret dont l'assise est de la résine polyester dans laquelle sont noyés les pieds et des anneaux en bambou. Le dessin du siège rappelle les cellules densément réparties d'un morceau de bambou vu au microscope. L'assise joue avec les tiges creuses qui permettent par ailleurs de saisir facilement le tabouret. Le motif formé d'inclusions de bambou renforce la solidité de la résine moulée. Ce tabouret pourrait sans problème être produit en série sans qu'il y en ait deux pareils à l'arrivée.

ESP
La Célula de bambú es un taburete con asiento de resina de poliéster en el que se han insertado patas de bambú con diversos anillos. El diseño del asiento recuerda a las células comprimidos en un trecho de bambú que se observan claramente a través del microscopio. Gracias a las patas huecas, es fácil cogerlo y levantarlo. El dibujo del bambú subraya la fuerza de la resina moldeada. Aunque el taburete se fabricara en masa, cada pieza sería única.

POR
A Célula de bambu é um tamborete com assento de resina de poliéster, no qual se inseriram pernas de bambu com certo número de anéis de bambu. O design do assento lembra as células densamente encaixadas de um pedaço de bambu, que se pode ver claramente quando se observa a planta pelo microscópio. A propriedade oca das pernas se manifesta no assento, e esta característica facilita que o tamborete seja fácil de apanhar e levantar. O desenho de bambu aumenta a força da resina moldada. O tamborete poderia ser facilmente produzido em série, embora cada peça ainda seria única.

BARCA

DESIGN FIRM
Jakob Joergensen

DESIGNER
Jakob Joergensen

PHOTOGRAPHY
Vanna Envall

CLIENT
Conde House Japan

Barca, designed by Jakob Joergensen, consists of boards that are shaped similarly to those used in boats. They can be moved independently of each other, and if heldtogether they create a changeable,spherical shape. The materials used to make Barca are laminated wood and a plastic joint that holds the boards together.

FRA
Barca, créé par Jakob Joergensen, est un ensemble de lattes recourbées ressemblant à celles utilisées pour les coques de bateau. Chacune peut être déplacée indépendamment des autres pour créer une sphère dont on peut modifier la configuration à tout moment. Les lattes sont en bois lamellé et sont assemblées avec des joints en plastique.

ESP
Barca, diseñado por Jakob Joergensen, consiste en una serie de tablones a los que se les da una forma semejante a los que se usan en las barcas. Se mueven independientemente unos de otros y cuando están juntos crean una forma cambiante y esférica. Los materiales empleados son madera laminada y una juntura de plástico que une los tablones.

POR
Barca, projetado por Jakob Joergensem, consiste em quadros aos quais se dá uma forma semelhante aos usados em barcos. Podem mover-se independentemente um de outro, e se mantêm juntos, criam uma forma mutável, esférica. Os materiais usados para fazer Barca são madeira laminada e uma junção de plástico que fixa os quadros.

FJARILL

DESIGN FIRM
Jakob Joergensen

DESIGNER
Jakob Joergensen

PHOTOGRAPHY
Vanna Envall

CLIENT
Galerie Maria Wettergren

Fjarill is a drawer system that is available from the Galerie Maria Wettergren in Paris. Through a rhythmical movement the draw system expands, transforming from a simple box into a functional sculpture as it does so. Fjarill is made from Oregon pine and a plastic joint that holds the drawers together at their corners.

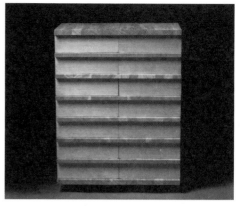

FRA

La commode Fjarill est un meuble à tiroirs proposé par la Galerie Maria Wettergren de Paris. Un glissement fait apparaître les tiroirs et transforme en sculpture fonctionnelle ce qui semblait être une simple caisse en bois. Fjarill est fabriquée en pin d'Orégon et les tiroirs sont retenus à un angle par un dispositif en plastique.

ESP

Fjarill es una cajonera disponible en la galería Maria Wettergren de Paris. La cajonera se expande mediante un movimiento rítmico, transformándose de este modo una simple caja en una escultura funcional. Está hecha de pino de Oregón y cuenta con una juntura de plástico que une las esquinas de los cajones.

POR

Fjarill é um sistema de gavetas, disponível na Galeria Maria Wettergrem de Paris. Através de um movimento rítmico, expande-se o sistema de gavetas, transformando deste modo uma simples caixa numa escultura funcional. Fjarill é feito de pinheiro do Óregon e uma junção de plástico que fixa as gavetas pelo canto.

BAUM

DESIGN FIRM
Jakob Joergensen

DESIGNER
Jakob Joergensen

PHOTOGRAPHY
Vanna Envall

CLIENT
Galerie Maria Wettergren

Baum is inspired by trees. Four trunks in a repeated pattern create a simple stool made from maple. The main question defining this work is how to create shapes consisting of smaller, repeated elements, or rather how to create in a simple and easy manner of production what seem like—in the sense of their organic quality, and in spite of having been composed of identical geometrical elements—complicated free shapes. Jakob Joergensen, the designer of Baum, is not so much interested in geometry as he is in shape in a more natural sense. Geometry has his interest as a productive method that can be used to create and give an overview of otherwise-complicated free forms.

FRA

L'arbre est la source d'inspiration du tabouret Baum. Quatre troncs suivant un motif répétitif forment le tabouret en érable. Ici, la question est comment créer des formes constituées de petits éléments qui se répètent ou plutôt, comment fabriquer facilement des formes d'apparence complexe, alors que l'on utilise un matériau naturel et des modules géométriques reproduits à l'identique. Ce qui intéresse Jakob Joergensen, le designer de Baum, n'est pas tant la géométrie que la forme en soi. Ici, la géométrie est une méthode de production qui permet de fabriquer sans peine des formes libres qu'il aurait été difficile de créer autrement.

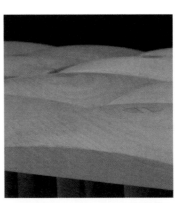

ESP

Baum se inspira en los árboles. Se trata de un sencillo taburete de arce compuesto de cuatro troncos que se repiten. La pregunta más importante a la hora de definir esta obra es cómo crear formas arbóreas complejas (en el sentido de sus cualidades orgánicas, aunque se compongan de elementos geométricos idénticos) mediante un proceso de fabricación sencillo. A Jakob Joergensen, el diseñador de Baum, la geometría solo le interesa como método productivo, con el que pueden crearse formas arbóreas complejas al tiempo que se ofrece una visión general de las mismas.

POR

Árvore inspira-se em árvores. Quatro troncos repetidos num modelo criam um simples tamborete feito de plátano. A questão principal que define esta obra é como criar formas que consistam em elementos menores e repetidos ou, melhor dito, como criar com uma forma de produção simples e fácil o que venham a parecer —no sentido de sua qualidade orgânica, e apesar de terem sido compostas por elementos geométricos idênticos— complicadas formas livres. Jakob Joergensem, o designer de Árvore, não está tão interessado na geometria como na forma, num sentido mais natural. A geometria tem seu interesse como método produtivo, que se pode usar para criar e dar uma visão geral de formas livres normalmente complicadas.

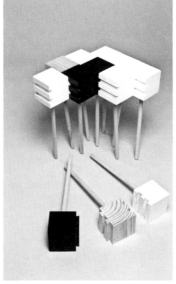

ENDLESS TABLE

DESIGN FIRM
Fabriq Studio

PHOTOGRAPHY
Barbara San Martin / Pilar Castro

DESIGNER
Wenchuman

It is a multi-shape table that can grow or shrink as needed according to the number of cubes used. Each of the cubes adds to or subtracts from the whole through an interlocking system. It was conceived to be as simple as possible, and is made for the most part from pine from local, renewable forests. The legs are made from tep a wood, which has a high level of mechanical resistance. The width of the cubes, the way they interlock, and the inclination of the legs all contribute to the structural stability of the table.

FRA
C'est une table protéiforme que l'on peut allonger ou raccourcir à volonté suivant le nombre de cubes utilisé. Les cubes s'emboîtent et se désemboîtent facilement, le système ayant été conçu pour un assemblage aussi simple que possible. La table est pratiquement tout en pin, matériau renouvelable provenant de forêts de la région. Les pieds sont en pinus taeda qui possède une excellente résistance mécanique. La largeur des cubes, ainsi que la manière dont ils s'emboîtent et l'inclinaison des pieds contribuent à la stabilité structurelle de la table.

ESP
Se trata de una mesa multiforme que se hace más grande o más pequeña en función de las necesidades según el número de cubos que se utilicen. Cada uno de ellos le añade o le resta algo al conjunto mediante un sistema de engranajes. Está diseñada para ser tan sencilla como sea posible y está hecha sobre todo de pino de bosques locales y renovables. Las patas son de madera de tepa, que tiene una gran resistencia mecánica. La anchura de los cubos, así como la manera en la que se estos se engranan, y la inclinación de las patas contribuyen a la estabilidad estructural de la mesa.

POR
A Mesa interminável foi desenhada para modernos ambientes de lar, que sobretudo necessitam flexibilidade para a otimização espacial. É uma mesa multiforme, que pode crescer ou encolher de acordo com a necessidade conforme o número de cubos usados. Cada cubo é adicionado ou retirado do conjunto através de um sistema de engrenagens. Foi concebido com a maior simplicidade possível, e é feito principalmente de pinheiro dos bosques locais e renováveis. As pernas são feitas de madeira de tepa, que tem um alto nível de resistência mecânica. A largura dos cubos, a forma como se entrelaçam e a inclinação das pernas contribuem para a estabilidade estrutural da mesa.

CLAMP CHAIR

DESIGNER
Andreas Kowalewski

PHOTOGRAPHY
Andreas Kowalewski

The goal for this design project was quite simple and almost trivial: the designer wanted to design and build a comfortable yet simple wooden chair that revealed the beauty of wood as a material and the skills of the craftsman. The approach taken was to create a modern wooden chair made in a traditional and conventional way. The designer wanted to articulate comfort and refined proportions, combining them with structural details such as the wooden joints, to emphasize the chair's appearance and precision. The chair frame is made out of oak or walnut and the upholstered seat and backrest come in different woven, coarse-mesh fabrics.

FRA
Fabriqué d'une seule pièce dans du contreplaqué moulé, le dossier capitonné enveloppe comme une coquille le corps de la personne qui s'y assoit. L'objectif de ce projet était des plus simples : le designer voulait concevoir et fabriquer une chaise en bois confortable qui mette en valeur la beauté naturelle du matériau et le travail de l'ébéniste. Il a décidé de créer une chaise moderne en bois façonnée suivant les méthodes traditionnelles, plutôt que d'explorer de nouveaux procédés de fabrication. Andreas Kowalewski souhaitait conjuguer confort avec élégance des proportions, tout en soignant les détails structurels comme les assemblages en bois, pour mettre en valeur l'esthétique et la sobriété de la forme. Le cadre de la chaise est en chêne et en noyer, et le capitonnage de l'assise et du dossier est disponible en différents tissus à mailles larges.

ESP
Fabricado con una sola plancha de madera contrachapada moldeada, el respaldo tapizado envuelve el cuerpo del usuario como si fuera una concha. El objetivo de este proyecto era muy sencillo y casi intrascendente: el artista quería diseñar y construir una silla de madera cómoda y sin embargo sencilla en la que se manifestara la belleza de la madera y la habilidad del artesano. Así, tomó la decisión de crear una silla de madera moderna, aunque fabricada de acuerdo con los métodos tradicionales y convencionales. Quería articular el confort y las proporciones refinadas, que combinaría con detalles estructurales como las junturas de madera, subrayando la imagen y la precisión de la silla. El armazón de la silla es de roble o nogal y tanto el asiento como el respaldo tapizados vienen en diferentes telas de malla gruesa.

POR
Feita a partir de uma só peça de compensado moldado, o apoio estofado abraça o corpo do usuário como uma concha. O objetivo deste projeto de design era muito simples e quase trivial: o designer queria projetar e construir uma cadeira de madeira cômoda e, no entanto, simples que revelasse a beleza da madeira como material e a habilidade do artesão. O foco escolhido foi criar uma cadeira moderna de madeira feita de forma tradicional e convencional, em vez de explorar novos processos de fabricação. O designer queria articular conforto e proporções refinadas, combinando com detalhes estruturais como as junções de madeira, para enfatizar a aparência e a precisão da cadeira. A estrutura da cadeira é feita de carvalho ou nogueira e o assento e apoio estofados vêm em diferentes tecidos de malha grossa entretecida.

SCHMÖBEL SHOE CABINET

DESIGNER
Andreas Kowalewski

PHOTOGRAPHY
Andreas Kowalewski

Schmöbel reinterprets the traditional concept of hallway furniture by offering a comfortable seated position to the user as he or she selects and changes shoes. The upholstered seat is seamlessly integrated into the oak corpus, which rests on a thin steel frame that makes the cabinet almost appear to be floating. Sufficient storage space for footwear can be found below the seat and to its right-and left-hand sides.

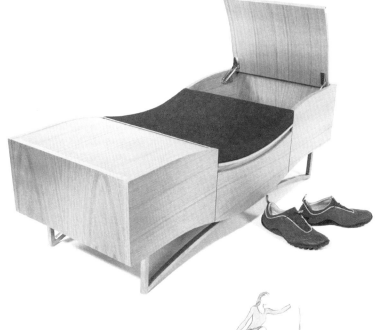

FRA

Il réinterprète à sa manière le meuble d'entrée traditionnel en offrant à l'utilisateur un endroit confortable où s'assoire pour ranger ou choisir ses chaussures. Le siège capitonné s'intègre parfaitement à la structure en chêne reposant sur un mince cadre en acier qui lui donne l'impression de flotter dans l'espace. De vastes espaces de rangement peuvent accueillir de nombreuses paires de chaussures, au-dessous, à droite et à gauche du siège.

ESP

El Schmöbel reinterpreta el concepto tradicional de mueble de pasillo. El asiento tapizado se integra a la perfección en el cuerpo de roble, que descansa sobre una delgada estructura de acero que hace que el zapatero parezca ingrávido. Encontrará un amplio espacio debajo del asiento, así como a ambos lados del mismo.

POR

Schmöbel reinterpreta o tradicional conceito de móvel de vestíbulo. O assento estofado está integrado de forma contínua no corpo de carvalho, que descansa sobre uma delgada estrutura de aço que faz com que o armário pareça estar quase flutuando. Pode-se encontrar espaço suficiente de armazenagem debaixo do assento e a sua direita e esquerda.

VIKA COFFEE TABLE

DESIGNER
Andreas Kowalewski

PHOTOGRAPHY
Andreas Kowalewski

The objective of this project was to create a three-dimensional structure from a flat sheet of metal, without using any additional parts or screws. The frame is made from just one sheet of stainless steel that has been laser cut and bent several times, and eventually transformed into a robust coffee-table construction. Each detail has its structural reason and defines the visual character of the table. This project explores the possibilities of laser-cutting manufacturing technology and the potential of steel.

FRA

Le but recherché ici était de créer une structure tridimensionnelle à partir d'une feuille de métal sans utiliser aucun autre élément ni vis. Le cadre est formé à partir d'une feuille en acier inoxydable découpée au laser et soumise à différents pliages. Le résultat est une table basse particulièrement solide. Chaque détail a une fonction structurelle et définit en même temps le « look » de la table. Ce projet explore les possibilités de la découpe au laser comme technologie de fabrication et le potentiel de l'acier.

ESP

El objetivo de este proyecto era crear una estructura tridimensional a partir de una lámina metálica, sin tornillos ni componentes adicionales. La estructura se basa en una plancha de acero inoxidable cortada con láser y doblada sucesivamente hasta transformarse en una robusta mesita de café. Cada detalle tiene una razón estructural y define el carácter estético de la mesa. El proyecto explora las posibilidades de la tecnología mediante el corte con láser y el potencial del acero.

POR

O objetivo deste projeto era criar uma estrutura tridimensional a partir de uma lâmina de metal, sem usar partes adicionais ou parafusos. A estrutura é feita a partir de uma só lâmina de aço inoxidável que foi cortada a laser e dobrada várias vezes e, finalmente, se transformou numa construção sólida de mesa para o café. Cada detalhe tem a sua razão estrutural e define o caráter visual da mesa. Este projeto explora as possibilidades da tecnologia de fabricação mediante o corte por laser e o potencial do aço.

ATLAS CHAIR

DESIGN FIRM
Jarvie-Design

DESIGNER
Scott Jarvie

PHOTOGRAPHY
Scott Jarvie

The Atlas project explores the possibilities of rationalizing complex surface geometries in a manner that resolves a number of the challenges associated with translating sculptural, computer-generated forms into constructible fundamentals. The Atlas Chair was derived by projecting flat-angled planes through a volume and using the intersecting elements to generate the profiles that create the sections of the chair. This allows complex surface geometry to be rationalized to planar surfaces, allowing sculptural possibilities while being material efficient and creating a system that facilitates construction.

FRA

Le projet Atlas explore les possibilités de rationalisation de surfaces géométriques complexes pour dégager certains principes de base s'appliquant à la fabrication d'objets à partir de formes générées par ordinateur. Atlas dérive de la projection d'angles plats sur un volume : les éléments d'intersection sont utilisés pour produire des profils correspondant aux sections de la chaise. Cette rationalisation permet d'identifier des possibilités volumétriques tout en définissant une utilisation optimale des matériaux et en créant un système facilitant la construction.

ESP

El proyecto Atlas explora las posibilidades de la racionalización de las geometrías superficiales complejas con el fin de superar ciertas dificultades que se asocian con la transformación de formas escultóricas generadas por ordenador en elementos de construcciòn. La silla Atlas surge proyectando planos en ángulo recto a través de un volumen y empleando los elementos secantes para generar las formas que crean las secciones de la silla. De esta forma se racionalizan las geometrías superficiales complejas, que se convierten en superficies planas con posibilidades escultóricas, al tiempo que se hace un uso eficiente de los materiales y se crea un sistema que facilita la construcción.

POR

O projeto Atlas explora as possibilidades de racionalizar as complexas geometrias de superfície, de tal forma a resolver certo número de desafios associados a transformar formas esculturais geradas por computador em fundamentos construtíveis. A cadeira Atlas surgiu ao projetar planos de ângulo plano através de um volume e usar os elementos que se cruzam para gerar os perfis que criam as seções da cadeira. Isto permite racionalizar complexas geometrias de superfície a superfícies planares, permitindo possibilidades esculturais, sendo ao mesmo tempo eficaz no material e criando um sistema que facilita a construção.

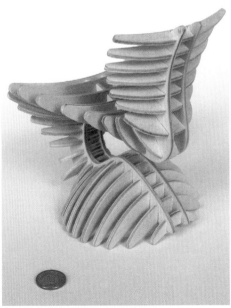

STAIRCASE

DESIGNER
Danny Kuo

PHOTOGRAPHY
Danny Kuo

The most efficient way to build is vertically. By focusing on height rather than width, efficient storage designs can be created. However, high storage designs can create a new problem because the higher storage parts are difficult to reach. Staircase is a shelving unit that combines a bookshelf with a pullout stair system in the bottom three shelves. The material chosen to make Staircase is bamboo because of both its look and its sustainable qualities.

FRA
La meilleure façon de construire est de procéder de bas en haut. C'est en se concentrant sur la hauteur au lieu de la largeur que l'on arrive à concevoir des meubles de rangement efficaces. Toutefois, à partir d'un certain point, la hauteur devient un handicap car on a du mal à accéder aux affaires rangées tout en haut. Le meuble Staircase combine l'idée de commode et d'escabeau : les trois premiers modules sont mobiles et on peut les utiliser comme marches pour accéder aux étagères du haut. Le bambou a été choisi pour fabriquer Staircase en raison de son aspect et de sa durabilité.

ESP
Lo más eficiente es construir hacia arriba. Al concentrarse en la altura en vez de la anchura, se crean espacios de almacenaje más eficaces. Sin embargo, es posible que los diseños más altos presenten un nuevo problema, dado que las secciones más elevadas quedan fuera de nuestro alcance. Escalera es una estantería en la que se combinan los estantes con una escalera extraíble en los tres estantes inferiores. Está hecha de bambú debido a la apariencia y las cualidades sostenibles de este.

POR
A forma mais eficaz de construir é verticalmente. Quando se centra na altura em vez da largura, podem-se criar eficazes designs de armazenagem. No entanto, os designs de armazenagem em altura podem criar um novo problema porque as partes mais altas da armazenagem são difíceis de alcançar. Escada é uma estante que combina estantes com um sistema de escada escamoteável nas três estantes inferiores. O material escolhido para fazer Escada é bambu devido à sua aparência e à sua natureza sustentável.

3×3

DESIGN FIRM
3PATAS

DESIGNER
Francesc Ros

PHOTOGRAPHY
Alicia Calle

3×3 is a collection of auxiliary tables that neatly combine to form a family. After researching different users, the designers found that in many cases they were living with limited space (for example in inner-city lofts) and were searching for solutions that could adapt to their various requirements. Whether entertaining friends, having a coffee, watching TV, or simply eating dinner, the adaptability of 3×3 makes the table an attractive solution for these users. The large, main table contains two smaller tables that users can remove and use independently. When the smaller tables are removed from the main one, two bowls fit perfectly in the spaces, modifying the functionality of the table. The table's design allows it to be easily transported, either during distribution or simply when moving house. The table legs can be effortlessly removed and the different elements easily boxed together.

FLEZI

DESIGN FIRM
Florian Saul Design Development

DESIGNER
Florian Saul & Eva Gerhards

PHOTOGRAPHY
Florian Saul & Eva Gerhard

Flezi is a chair that is characterized by its organic and dynamic shape. It provides a relaxed, ground-level seat and is very versatile due to its lightweight design. Its Belmadur® treatment enables the Flezi chair to be used indoors and outdoors.

FRA
Flezi est une chaise dont la forme particulière combine l'esthétique naturelle du matériau et l'aérodynamisme. Elle offre une assise confortable au niveau du sol et est à l'aise partout grâce à sa légèreté aérienne. Traitée au Belmadur®, elle peut être utilisée aussi bien à l'intérieur qu'à l'extérieur.

ESP
Flezi es una silla con una forma orgánica y dinámica característica que ofrece un asiento confortable al nivel del suelo y es tan liviana que tiene muchas posibilidades. Gracias al tratamiento con Belmadur® puede instalarse tanto en interiores como en exteriores.

POR
Flezi é uma cadeira caracterizada por sua forma orgânica e dinâmica. Proporciona um assento relaxado ao nível do solo e é muito versátil devido o seu design leve. Seu tratamento com Belmadur® permite que a cadeira Flezi seja usada tanto em interiores como em exteriores.

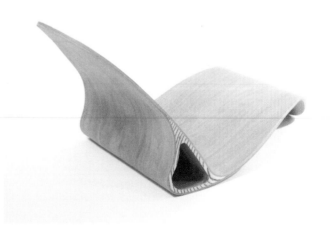

SHEEP CHAIR

DESIGN FIRM
Ag Studio

DESIGNER
Tzu-Chi, Yin

PHOTOGRAPHY
Tzu-Chi, Yin

CLIENT
CHO CHIA TING MUFFLER CO.,LTD

Sheep are associated with feelings of comfort and softness, and people often want to touch them, play with them, and bring them home. Therefore by using the form of a sheep this piece of furniture creates that atmosphere of warmth in the home. One special characteristic of the Sheep Chair is the space on its top surface for holding small objects such as remote controls or magazines, helping you to keep your personal space tidy. And the Sheep Chair's towel covering makes for a very comfortable sitting experience.

ESP
Las ovejas nos inspiran sensaciones cómodas y suaves y mucha gente desea tocarlas, jugar con ellas y hasta llevárselas a casa. Así pues, al basarse en la forma de una oveja, este mueble crea una atmósfera cálida en el hogar. Una curiosa característica de la Silla de oveja es que la superficie dispone de un espacio donde se guardan objetos pequeños, como revistas o mandos a distancia, contribuyendo a que los espacios personales estén ordenados. Y el forro de felpa proporciona una experiencia sumamente confortable.

POR
As ovelhas são associadas com sensações de comodidade e suavidade, e as pessoas frequentemente querem tocar nelas, brincar com elas e levá-las para casa. Portanto, ao usar a forma de uma ovelha, este móvel cria uma atmosfera cálida no lar. Uma caracteristica especial da Cadeira Ovelha é o espaço em sua superfície para alojar pequenos objetos, como controles remotos ou revistas, lhe ajudando a manter seu espaço pessoal arrumado. E a cobertura com toalha da Cadeira Ovelha proporciona uma experiência de assento muito cômodo.

FRA
Ces ovidés représentent le confort et la douceur ; les gens ont souvent envie de les toucher, de jouer avec eux, voire, de les ramener à la maison ! Ainsi, le tabouret « mouton » crée une ambiance cosy chez soi. Une des particularités du tabouret Sheep est que son coussin est muni de logements destinés à accueillir des petits objets, comme une télécommande, un magazine, etc. Votre espace personnel sera ainsi toujours net et bien rangé. Le tissu éponge qui recouvre l'assise assure un confort extrême à l'utilisateur.

HUSH

DESIGN FIRM
Freyja

DESIGNER
Freyja Sewell

Using 100 percent wool felt, HUSH creates an enclosed space, providing a personal retreat and an escape into a dark, hushed, natural space in the midst of a busy airport, office, shop, or library. HUSH can also be transformed to provide more traditional, open seating. Wool is naturally flame retardant, breathable, durable, and elastic; it is also multiclimatic, meaning it is warm when the environment is cold and cool when it's warm. It is of course also biodegradable and so won't clog up a landfill after disposal.

FRA
Fabriqué à partir de feutre pur laine, HUSH permet de créer un espace clos, un recoin isolé, sombre et naturel qui étouffe les bruits au beau milieu d'un aéroport, d'un bureau, d'une boutique ou d'une bibliothèque bondés. HUSH peut aussi s'ouvrir pour se transformer en fauteuil plus classique. La laine est une matière naturellement résistante à la flamme, perméable à l'air, durable et adaptée à tous les climats : elle tient chaud quand il fait froid et garde au frais quand il fait chaud. La laine est bien sûr biodégradable et n'encombrera pas la décharge le jour où on se débarrassera du fauteuil.

ESP
Empleando fieltro de lana 100%, SILENCIO crea un espacio cerrado, ofreciéndonos un refugio privado y una huida a un espacio oscuro, apacible y natural en medio de un aeropuerto concurrido, una oficina, una tienda o una biblioteca. SILENCIO también se transforma en un asiento abierto más tradicional. La lana es naturalmente resistente al fuego, transpirable, duradera y elástica; además es multiclimática, lo que significa que es cálida cuando hace frío y fresca cuando hace calor. Por supuesto, también es biodegradable, de modo que cuando se tira no se amontona en ningún vertedero.

POR
Usando feltro 100 % de lã, SILÊNCIO cria um espaço fechado, proporcionando um retiro pessoal e um escape para o espaço escuro, silencioso e natural no meio de um aeroporto concorrido, escritório, loja ou biblioteca. SILÊNCIO também pode transformar-se a fim de proporcionar um assento mais tradicional, aberto. A lã é naturalmente resistente ao fogo, transpirável, durável e elástica; também é multiclimática, o que significa que é quente quando o ambiente é frio e fresca quando faz calor. Naturalmente, também é biodegradável e, por isso, depois de descartá-la, não obstruirá um aterro sanitário.

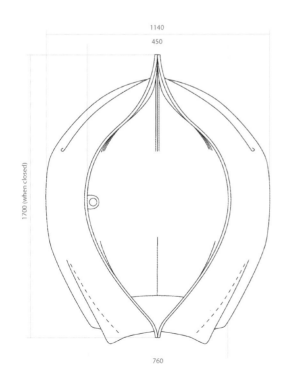

1140

450

1700 (when closed)

760

STACKABLE
DESK/BED...?

BED?

LIVINGSTONES

DESIGN FIRM
smarin

DESIGNER
Stephanie Marin

PHOTOGRAPHY
Stephanie Marin

Designed by Stephanie Marin, Livingstones pebble cushions are upholstered in pure virgin wool. The cushions are made using nonallergenic polysilicon fibers, and the seats are based around a highly comfortable structure made from Bultex foam rubber. Being French manufactured, of the highest quality, and environmentally friendly—Livingstones are made entirely from pure, natural materials, with the wool mineral dye shaving been produced without the use of chemicals—all guarantee that Livingstones provide remarkable comfort and an exceptional longevity.

POR
Desenhadas por Stephanie Marin, as almofadas de seixos rolados Pedras viventes são estofadas com pura lã virgem. As almofadas são feitas usando fibras de polisilicone não alergênicas, e os assentos baseiam-se numa estrutura muito cômoda feita de borracha de espuma Bultex. Sendo fabricadas na França, da mais alta qualidade e favoráveis ao meio ambiente, Pedras viventes são feitas totalmente de materiais puros e naturais, com os corantes minerais da lã produzidos sem uso de agentes químicos —tudo garante que as Pedras viventes proporcionem uma comodidade extraordinária e uma longevidade excepcional.

FRA
Conçus par Stéphanie Marin, les coussins galets Livingstones sont recouverts d'une housse en pure laine vierge. Ils sont fabriqués en fibres polysilicones non allergènes. Leur assise est constituée d'une structure très confortable en caoutchouc mousse Bultex. Les coussins Livingstones sont fabriqués en France. Ils sont de très haute qualité et respectent l'environnement. Ils sont élaborés entièrement à partir de matériaux naturels, les colorants minéraux pour la laine ne contenant aucun produit chimique. Toute ceci garantit que les coussins Livingstones procurent un remarquable confort et ont une longévité exceptionnelle.

ESP
Los cojines de guijarros Piedras vivas de Stephanie Marin están hechos con fibras de polisilicona no alergénicas y tapizados con pura lana virgen. Los asientos se basan en una estructura muy confortable de gomaespuma Bultex. La manufactura francesa, la calidad y el respeto al medioambiente (están hechas con materiales puros y naturales, con los tintes minerales de la lana que se producen sin agentes químicos) garantizan que las Piedras vivas sean notablemente cómodas y extraordinariamente duraderas.

LE HASARD

DESIGN FIRM
smarin

DESIGNER
Stephanie Marin

PHOTOGRAPHY
Stephanie Marin

Le Hasard is a combination of a bench, a worktop, and two shelves. It can be used either as a whole set or as three separate elements that can be arranged as you wish. It is a space, shapes, colors, and rhythms, all of which are eager to express their freedom. It is a set of storage furniture, a tower, a folding screen, a coffee table, a bench, a worktop, a desk, shelves, and a bookcase. It is a whole mobile set; a room by itself. It has neither a side nor a bottom, you can see it from any angle.

FRA
Le Hasard est un ensemble composé d'un banc, d'une table et de deux étagères. On peut regrouper les trois modules ou bien les dissocier, suivant sa préférence. L'espace, les formes, les couleurs et les rythmes se conjuguent pour former un meuble de rangement, une tour, un paravent pliant, une table basse, un banc, un plan de travail, un bureau, des étagères et une bibliothèque. Le Hasard n'a ni base ni côté, et on peut le voir sous tous les angles.

ESP
El Azar combina un banco con una superficie de trabajo y dos estanterías. Puede usarse conjuntamente o como tres elementos independientes que se disponen al gusto del usuario. Es un conjunto de muebles de almacenaje, una torre, una pantalla plegable, una mesita de café, un banco, una superficie de trabajo y un escritorio, así como estantes y una librería. No tiene ni lados ni fondo y puede verse desde todos los ángulos.

POR
O Acaso é a combinação de um banco, uma superfície de trabalho e duas estantes. Pode ser usado como um conjunto total ou como três elementos separados que se podem colocar como se deseje. É um conjunto de móveis de armazenagem, uma torre, uma tela que se dobra, uma mesa de café, um banco, uma superfície de trabalho, um escritório, estantes e uma livraria. Não tem nem lados nem fundo, pode ser visto de qualquer ângulo.

16/45
END TABLE

DESIGN FIRM
Uhuru

PHOTOGRAPHY
Uhuru

The 16/45 End Tables vary in size, each referencing the colossal diameter and caliber of the bullets that were onboard the USS North Carolina. The tapered shape of the table supports took subtle cues from the battleship itself. The lightness of the base is a direct contrast to the solid bullets. Crafted out of either teak or cold-rolled steel, the tables have black-glass tops and are available in three heights.

FRA

Les tables d'extrêmité 16/45 existent en différentes tailles, chacune représentant le diamètre et le calibre des obus qu'il y avait à bord du navire USS North Carolina. La forme élancée des pieds est une allusion à la coque du bateau de guerre. La légèreté de la base contraste avec la masse des obus. Les tables, fabriquées en teck ou en acier laminé à froid, disposent d'un plateau en verre fumé et existent en trois hauteurs.

ESP

Las mesitas auxiliares 16/45 tienen distintos tamaños, puesto que cada una de ellas hace referencia al diámetro y el calibre colosales de los proyectiles que se encontraban a bordo del acorazado USS North Carolina. La forma en la que se estrechan los soportes se inspira sutilmente en el propio buque de guerra. La base liviana ofrece un claro contraste con los robustos proyectiles. Estas mesitas de teca o acero laminado en frío tienen una superficie de cristal oscuro y están disponibles en tres alturas.

POR

As Mesinhas auxiliares 16/45 variam em tamanho, cada uma faz referência ao diâmetro e calibre colossais dos projéteis que estavam a bordo do USS North Carolina. A forma como se vão estreitando os suportes da mesa tomaram pistas sutis do próprio navio de guerra. A leveza da base está em vivo contraste com os sólidos projéteis. Esculpidas em teca ou em aço laminado a frio, as mesinhas têm superfícies de vidro escuro e estão disponíveis em três alturas.

CYCLONE LOUNGER

DESIGN FIRM
Uhuru

PHOTOGRAPHY
Uhuru

The Cyclone roller coaster is one of Coney Island's last-remaining functional rides. It is resurrected here in the form of a lounge chair, with a crisp-white, laser-cut metal base. Uhuru plays off the organized chaos of the ride's structure, flattened to one layer of metal, and with the sides connected sporadically to create a dynamic interchange of space and void on the base. The metal is finished with a low-VOCpowder-coat finish.

FRA
Les montagnes russes Cyclone font partie des dernières attractions du parc de Coney Island qui fonctionnent encore. Elles nous ont servi d'inspiration ici pour créer cette chaise longue reposant sur un socle blanc découpé au laser. Uhuru s'amuse à reproduire la forêt de tiges qui semblent partir en tous sens pour former la structure. Les baguettes métalliques sont aplaties et reliées entres-elles par endroits de manière à créer une dynamique entre les pleins et les vides de l'espace occupé par le socle. Le métal est recouvert de peinture poudre à faible COV.

ESP
La montaña rusa Ciclón, una de las últimas atracciones en activo de Coney Island, ha resucitado en forma de tumbona, con una inmaculada base metálica blanca cortada con láser. Uhuru se enfrenta al caos organizado de la estructura de la montaña rusa, adoptando la forma lisa de una capa metálica con lados que se conectan esporádicamente y creando un intercambio dinámico de espacio y vacío en la base. El metal cuenta con un acabado de pintura electrostática baja en VOC.

POR
A montanha russa Ciclone é uma das últimas viagens funcionais que ficam em Coney Island. Ressuscitou aqui em forma de espreguiçadeira, com uma base branca imaculada de metal cortado a laser. Uhuru enfrenta o caos organizado da estrutura da montanha russa, aplanada a uma camada de metal, e com os lados conectados esporadicamente para criar um intercâmbio dinâmico de espaço e vazio na base. O metal está acabado com pintura eletrostática baixa em VOC.

MARBELOUS

DESIGN FIRM
Ontwerpduo

DESIGNERS
Tineke Beunders & Nathan Wierink

PHOTOGRAPHY
Ontwerpduo & Lisa Klappe

Tineke Beunders, codesigner of Marbelous, is aware that the worlds of adult furniture and children's toys are separate from one another. Nevertheless, from her childhood she remembered it was always exciting to combine the two, and used to use carved-wood furniture as a playing field for her puppets. With this experience in mind she and Nathan Wierink created a concept for a new piece of furniture. They designed functional woodcarvings—decorations you can play with—and applied them to a piece of furniture, thus combining the world of adults with the world of the children. A marble track in a table: a new type of woodcarving that invites you to play…

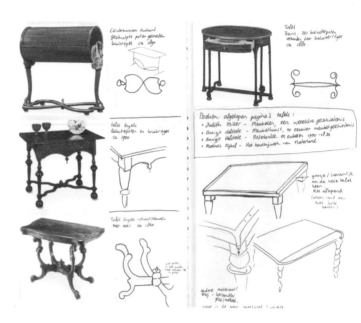

FRA

Tineke Beunders, cocréatrice de Marbelous, sait bien que le monde des meubles pour adultes n'a rien à voir avec celui des jouets d'enfants. Elle se rappelle pourtant que dans son enfance, elle s'amusait à combiner les deux, et transformait les beaux meubles de la maison en terrain de jeu pour ses poupées. Forte de cette expérience, elle a créé avec Nathan Wierink un nouveau concept de meuble. Ils ont conçu des sculptures en bois fonctionnelles — des décorations avec lesquelles on peut jouer — qu'ils ont intégrées à un meuble. Le résultat est un objet mariant le monde des adultes et celui des enfants. Il y a, par exemple, une piste pour les billes gravées sur le plateau de la table, qui invite à jouer…

ESP

Tineke Beunders, codiseñadora de Marbelous, es consciente de que los mundos de los muebles adultos y los juguetes infantiles están separados. Sin embargo, recuerda que cuando era niña le divertía combinarlos y que usaba los muebles de madera como campo de juego de sus muñecas. Con esta experiencia en mente, Nathan Wierink y ella han creado un nuevo concepto de mueble, diseñando tallas de madera funcionales (adornos con los que se puede jugar) y aplicándolas a un mueble, combinando de esta forma el mundo de los adultos y el de los niños. Una pista de canicas en una mesa: un nuevo tipo de talla que invita a al juego…

POR

Tineke Beunders, codesigner de Marbelous, está consciente de que os mundos de mobiliário adulto e do brinquedo infantil estão separados. No entanto, desde a infância ela lembra que sempre era divertido combiná-los e costumava usar móveis de madeira talhada como campo de brincadeiras para suas bonecas. Com esta experiência em mente, ela e Nathan Wierink criaram um conceito para um novo móvel. Desenharam madeira talhada funcional —decorações com as quais você brincar— e a aplicaram a um móvel, combinando assim o mundo dos adultos com o mundo das crianças. Um caminho de bolas de gude numa mesa: um novo tipo de madeira talhada que lhe convida a brincar, etc.

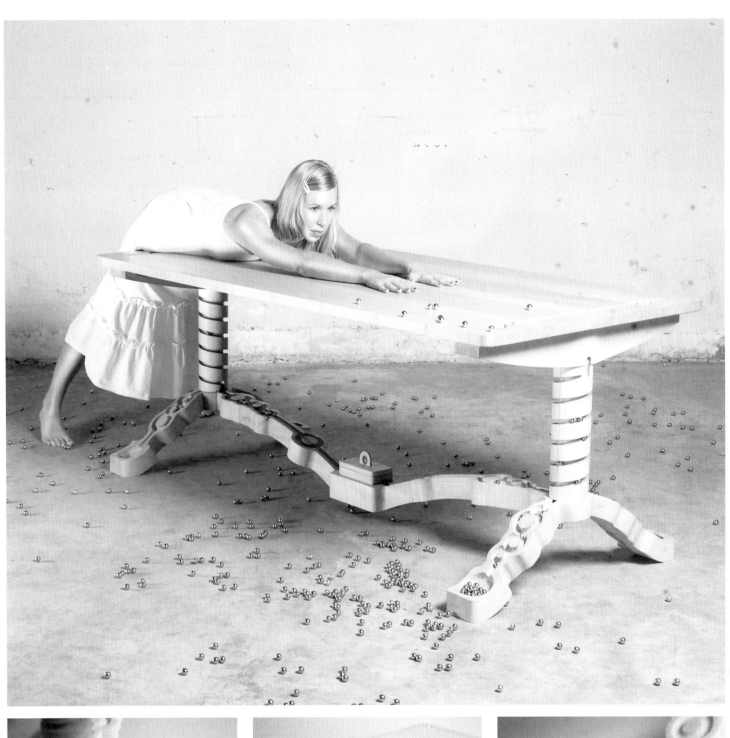

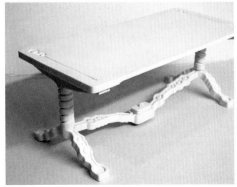
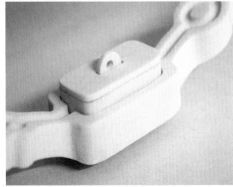

ZEED

DESIGN FIRM
Sara Leonor

DESIGNER
Sara Leonor

PHOTOGRAPHY
Sean Pines,
Jorge Güil & Daniel Hernandez

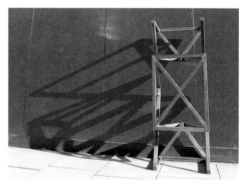

The chair was Sara Leonor's source of inspiration to create sculptural volumes from a union of individual units and a series of rigorous geometrical patterns. From these elements she created Zeed, her first piece of functional art, which was displayed at Tent London 2010.Zeed has meaning in two dimensions. From a personal perspective, the Zeed is the seed that will hopefully allow this designer to cultivate a career in the world of design. From a creative point of view, the chair intends to replicate a plant's ability to grow when stacked while keeping its functionality in isolation. A single Zeed is six hundred millimeters wide, five hundred millimeters deep, and eight hundred millimeters high.

FRA

Comme type de meuble, Sara Leonor a choisi le fauteuil pour créer des volumes sculpturaux à partir d'un assemblage de barreaux et de motifs géométriques stricts. C'est ainsi qu'elle a créé Zeed, sa première œuvre d'art fonctionnelle qui a été exposée à la foire Tent London 2010. Zeed a aussi un sens en deux dimensions : au niveau personnel, Zeed est la petite graine qui permettra sans aucun doute à cette artiste de faire carrière dans le monde du design. Sur le plan créatif, le fauteuil reproduit la manière dont poussent les plantes lorsqu'on en empile plusieurs, tout en restant parfaitement fonctionnel.
Un seul fauteuil Zeed mesure 60 cm de largeur pour une profondeur de 50 cm et une hauteur de 80 cm.

ESP

Sara Leonor se ha inspirado en la silla para crear volúmenes escultóricos basados en la unión de unidades individuales y una serie de estrictos patrones geométricos. Con estos elementos ha creado Zeed, su primera obra de arte funcional, que se exhibió en Tent, Londres, en 2010. Zeed tiene dos dimensiones de significado. Desde una perspectiva personal, Zeed es la semilla con la que esta diseñadora confía en cultivar una carrera en el mundo del diseño. Desde un punto de vista creativo, las sillas reproducen el crecimiento de las plantas cuando están apiladas, al tiempo que conservan sus funciones por separado. Una Zeed mide 600 ml de ancho, 500 ml de ancho y 800 ml de alto.

POR

A cadeira foi a fonte de inspiração de Sara Leonor para criar volumes esculturais a partir de uma união de unidades individuais e uma série de padrões geométricos rigorosos. A partir destes elementos, criou Zeed, sua primeira peça de arte funcional, que foi apresentada em Tent, Londres 2010. Zeed tem significado em duas dimensões. A partir de uma perspectiva pessoal, Zeed é a semente que esperemos e que permite a esta designer cultivar uma carreira no mundo do design. Do ponto de vista criativo, a cadeira pretende replicar a capacidade de uma planta crescer quando está empilhada, ao mesmo tempo em que mantém sua funcionalidade em isolamento. Uma só Zeed é 600 ml de largura, 500 ml de largura e 800 ml de alto.

3 BLOCKS

DESIGN FIRM
Kalon Studios

DESIGNERS
Johannes Pauwen & Michaele Simmering

CLIENT
Kalon Studios

3 Blocks is a set of three nesting tables/ stools that play with the elemental shapes of the square, the circle, and the line. The optional fern engraving is different on each of the three cubes. With lifelike precision the fern wraps around the edges, playfully overrunning the piece. Native to the Bamboo Sea in China, FSC-certified bamboo is a fastgrowing, natural material, not to mention lightweight and a strong wood substitute. Both the bamboo and the wood finish they use are recyclable, renewable, and biodegradable.

FRA
3 Blocks est un ensemble de 3 tables/ tabourets gigognes qui jouent avec les formes élémentaires du carré, du cercle et de la droite. La gravure de la fougère, disponible en option, est différente pour chacun des trois cubes. La fougère s'enroule avec réalisme autour des cubes comme si elle allait envahir l'espace. Originaire de la mer de bambou en Chine, le bambou certifié FSC est une plante à croissance rapide. Ce matériau naturel, particulièrement léger et solide, est un parfait substitut du bois. Le bambou ainsi que le vernis à bois utilisés sont recyclables, renouvelables et biodégradables.

ESP
3 Bloques es un conjunto de tres taburetes o mesas nido que juegan con las formas elementales del cuadrado, el círculo y la línea. Los grabados de helechos opcionales son diferentes en cada uno de los tres cubos. Con una precisión natural, el helecho envuelve los bordes, desbordando jovialmente la pieza. Originario del mar de Bambú, en China, el bambú con certificado del FSC es un material natural que crece muy deprisa; asimismo es liviano y un robusto sustituto de la madera. Tanto el bambú como el acabado de madera son reciclables, renovables y biodegradables.

POR
3 Blocos é um conjunto de três mesas/ tamboretes aninhados que jogam com as formas elementares do quadrado, do círculo e da linha. A gravação opcional de samambaia é diferente em cada um dos três cubos. Com uma precisão natural, a samambaia envolve as bordas, ultrapassando a peça alegremente. Originário do Mar de Bambu na China, o bambu com certificado FSC é um material natural que cresce rápidamente. Tanto o bambu como o acabamento de madeira que utilizam são recicláveis, renováveis e biodegradáveis.

WOODEN HAMMOCK

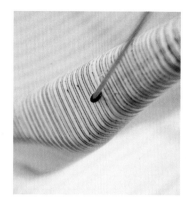

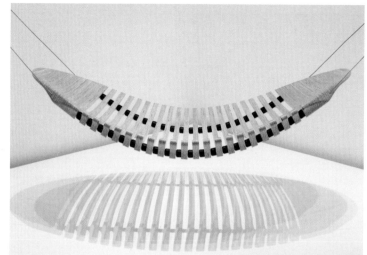

DESIGNER
Adam Cornish

PHOTOGRAPHY
Adam Cornish

The Wooden Hammock was designed as an alternative to the common cloth hammock. Although made from wood, the design is flexible and comfortable due to the rubber vertebra, which allows the wooden segments to move, mimicking the human spine. The segmented construction not only allows for flexibility and comfort but also prevents the collection of debris and water commonly associated with cloth hammocks. This feature means no more going out to lie in your hammock only to find a puddle of water and leaves.

Le hamac Wooden Hammock a été conçu comme alternative au modèle en toile. Bien qu'il soit fait en bois, sa forme est particulièrement souple et confortable grâce aux articulations en caoutchouc qui permettent aux segments de se mouvoir à la manière des vertèbres de la colonne vertébrale. Cette structure articulée assure non seulement souplesse et confort, mais évite que les saletés ou l'eau s'y accumulent comme dans les hamacs en toile : vous pouvez donc vous y allonger directement sans crainte.

A Rede de madeira foi concebida como alternativa à típica rede de tecido. Embora seja feita de madeira, o design é flexível e cômodo devido às vértebras de borracha, que permitem que os segmentos de madeira se movam, imitando a espinha humana. A construção segmentada não só permite flexibilidade e conforto, mas, além disso, evita recolher de restos e água que habitualmente se associam às redes de tecido. Esta caracteristica significa que já não vai sair para se deitar em sua rede e descobrir um charco de água e folhas.

Esta hamaca se ha concebido como alternativa a la típica hamaca de tela. Aunque está hecha de madera, el diseño es flexible y cómodo gracias a las vértebras elásticas, que permiten que los listones se desplacen, imitando a la columna humana. Además, la construcción en forma de segmentos impide que se acumulen los detritos y el agua que suelen asociarse con las hamacas de tela, de modo que nunca descubrirá un charco de agua y hojas cuando se tumbe en ella.

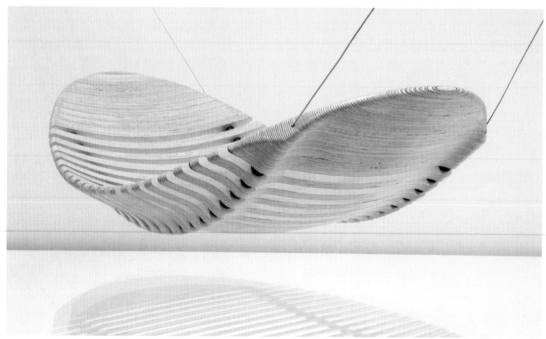

ALVISILKCHAIR

DESIGN FIRM
alvidesign

DESIGNER
Åsa Alvi Karolina Kärner

PHOTOGRAPHY
Kristin Montagu-Evans.

The alvisilkchair is a piece of environmentally friendly seating made from silk thread tightened around a bearing oak frame. The focal point of the chair is its transparency, which creates new forms and brings forth a perception of weightlessness, while the light produces new shadow plays from the alvisilkchair's threadwork. Long-staple silk is an extremely strong and durablenatural fiber, as demonstrated by the fact that there are very old and well-preserved qin instruments still in existence today. These qualities and the fact that silk also has a relatively low environmental impact explainthe designer's choice of the material for her alvisilkchair.

FRA
La chaise alvisilkchair est un siège écologique sympathique fabriqué à partir de fils en soie tendus sur un cadre en chêne. La qualité première d'alvisilkchair est sa transparence qui génère de nouvelles formes et donne une impression de légèreté, alors que la lumière joue à la cachette avec les ombres des fils. La soie à fibres longues est particulièrement solide et durable, comme le démontrent les qins conservés jusqu'à nos jours et qui ont toujours leurs cordes de l'époque. Pour l'alvisilkchair, la créatrice a choisi la soie pour ses qualités et son faible impact environnemental.

ESP
La alvisilkchair es una silla respetuosa con el medioambiente, fabricada con hilos de seda que se tensan en torno a una estructura de carga de roble. El punto focal de la misma es la transparencia, que crea formas novedosas y transmite una sensación de ingravidez, al tiempo que la luz produce juegos de sombras a través del tejido. La seda es una fibra natural extremadamente fuerte y duradera, como demuestra el hecho de que todavía hoy se conservan qin muy antiguos en buen estado. Estas cualidades, así como el impacto relativamente bajo de la seda en el medio ambiente, justifican la elección de la diseñadora para la alvisilkchair.

POR
A alvisilkchair é um assento favorável ao meio ambiente, feito de fio de seda esticado numa estrutura de carvalho que suporta o peso. O ponto focal da cadeira é a sua transparência, que cria novas formas e uma percepção de ausência de gravidade, ao mesmo tempo em que a luz produz novos jogos de sombras do tecido da alvisilkchair. A seda de fibra longa é uma fibra natural extremamente forte e durável, como fica demonstra pelo fato de que ainda hoje existam instrumentos qin muito antigos e bem conservados. Estas qualidades e o fato de que a seda também tem um impacto ambiental relativamente baixo explicam a escolha do material por parte da designer para seu alvisilkchair.

LOOPITA

DESIGN FIRM
Victor Alemán Estudio

Loopita is a unique design that takes seating a step further. It is more than just a conversation piece; it has been conceived as a space where people can interact with each other. It is a semi-intimate lounge for two. Its two opposing ends make a floor-level chaise. Made from birch plywood and covered with high-density foam for maximum comfort, it looks sleek and elegant, with a little bit of posh.

FRA

Le design de Loopita est unique en son genre : il redéfinit à lui seul la fonction du siège. Loopita est bien plus qu'une « commodité de la conversation ». Ce meuble a été conçu de manière à créer un espace où deux personnes peuvent interagir librement. C'est une sorte d'abri où l'on s'isole à deux. Ses deux extrémités, qui reposent à plat sur le sol, servent de chaises longues. Loopita est fabriquée en contreplaqué de bouleau et ses coussins sont en mousse haute densité pour un confort maximum. Le meuble est à la fois chic et élégant.

ESP

Loopita es un diseño único que trasciende el concepto de asiento. Es más que un simple espacio para la conversación; está concebido para que los usuarios interactúen. Se trata de una tumbona semiíntima para dos. Los dos extremos opuestos componen un diván al nivel del suelo. Fabricada con madera contrachapada de abedul y cubierta con espuma de alta densidad para ofrecer el máximo confort, tiene una estética elegante y hasta un aire lujoso.

POR

Loopita é um design único que ultrapassa o ato de se sentar. É mais do que uma peça de conversação; foi desenhada como um espaço onde a gente pode interagir. É uma espreguiçadeira semi-íntima para dois. Suas duas alas opostas fazem um divã ao nível do solo. Feita a partir de compensado de abeto e coberta com espuma de alta densidade para um conforto máximo, mostra-se elegante, inclusive com um ar luxuoso.

CHAISE LONGUE NO.4

DESIGN FIRM
Tom Raffield Design

DESIGNER
Tom Raffield

PHOTOGRAPHY
Dave Mann

Chaise Longue No.4 has been made using sustainably sourced, local English Oak that is steam bent into shape using Tom Raffield's cutting-edge bending techniques. Chaise Longue No.4 is as much a piece of art as it is a functional seat. It becomes a true showpiece in any environment, demonstrating how wood can be used to make such complex yet beautiful three-dimensional forms.

FRA

La Chaise Longue No.4 est fabriquée à partir d'un matériau durable, le chêne anglais de la région. Le bois est soumis à un cintrage à la vapeur suivant les techniques mises au point par Tom Raffield. La chaise longue est à la fois une œuvre d'art et un siège fonctionnel. Elle devient le centre d'attention quel que soit l'environnement où on la place. Elle est la preuve que le bois permet de créer des objets tridimensionnels complexes et esthétiques.

ESP

La Chaise Longue n.º 4 está hecha de roble inglés de origen sostenible, moldeado al vapor empleando las innovadoras técnicas de Tom Raffield. La Chaise Longue n.º 4 es una obra de arte al tiempo que un asiento funcional que se convierte en una auténtica atracción en todos los ambientes, ejemplificando el uso de la madera en la creación de formas tridimensionales complejas y sin embargo hermosas.

POR

A Chaise Longue n.º 4 foi construída usando carvalho inglês local, de origem sustentável, que se dobra por vapor usando as inovadoras técnicas de dobragem de Tom Raffield. A Chaise Longue n.º 4 é tanto uma peça de arte como um assento funcional. Converte-se num autêntico troféu em qualquer ambiente, demonstrando como se pode usar a madeira para criar estas formas tridimensionais complexas, mas preciosas.

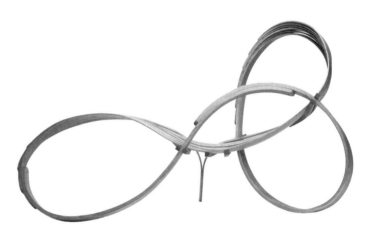

KAGUYA-HIME

DESIGN FIRM
designstudio Lotte van Laatum

DESIGNER
Lotte van Laatum

PHOTOGRAPHY
Thomas Fasting

CLIENT
Bamboolabs

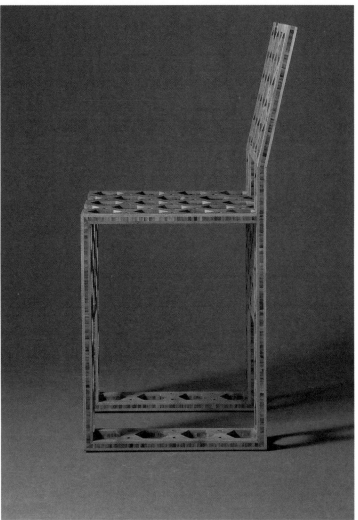

Kaguya-hime, which literally means "shining princess of the supple bamboo," is an ancient Japanese legend. This chair is based on this story and is an enlargement of the pattern of the woven basket in which Kaguya-hime grows up. The chair has been produced using a two-dimensional milling pattern, translating a traditional pattern into a Western style. The chair is made from a twenty-millimeter thick, three-layered sheet of bamboo.

FRA
Kaguya-hime, qui signifie « lumineuse princesse du souple bambou », est un ancien conte japonais. Le dessin de la chaise, qui s'inspire du conte, est une version agrandie du panier en bambou dans lequel Kaguya-hime a grandi. Il reproduit en deux dimensions le motif traditionnel occidentalisé. La chaise est fabriquée dans des panneaux en bambou d'une épaisseur de vingt millimètres constitués de trois plis.

ESP
Kaguya-hime, que literalmente significa "radiante princesa del bambú flexible", es la protagonista de una antigua leyenda japonesa. La silla se inspira en esta historia y amplía el diseño de la cesta en la que crece Kaguya-hime. Se basa en un diseño de molinillo en dos dimensiones en el que se transforma el modelo tradicional al estilo de Occidente. Está hecha con una plancha de bambú de tres capas y veinte milímetros de grosor.

POR
Kaguya-hime, que literalmente significa "princesa resplandecente do bambu flexível", é uma antiga lenda japonesa. A cadeira baseia-se nesta história e é uma ampliação do modelo de cesta entretecida na qual cresce Kaguya-hime. A cadeira foi produzida usando um padrão de cordãozinho bidimensional, transformando um modelo tradicional num estilo ocidental. A cadeira é feita de uma lâmina de bambu de vinte milímetros de espessura e três camadas.

E.I.S

DESIGN FIRM
Freyja

DESIGNER/ PHOTOGRAPHER
Freyja Sewell

E.I.S (Exercise In Simplicity) is a stool that follows two rules: firstly that it be made as simply as possible, thereby keeping production costs to a minimum; and secondly that it be made exclusively from bamboo, an immensely versatile material due to its incredible strength, beauty, low cost, and naturally occurring tubular shape. E.I.S combines modern bamboo laminate and bamboo fabric with natural bamboo tubes. It features absolutely no other materials or added glue or nails. Instead, the design of the joints exploits bamboo's innate properties. The stool (without cushion) is made of only three different, shaped components, a total of seven pieces, all made from 100 percent bamboo. The glue used in the production of the laminate is also biodegradable.

FRA

E.I.S (Exercise in Simplicity) est un tabouret qui suit deux règles. La première : qu'il soit fabriqué de la manière la plus simple possible pour réduire au minimum les coûts de production. La seconde : qu'il soit fait uniquement en bambou, qui est un matériau polyvalent à la fois solide, beau, bon marché et de forme naturelle tubulaire. E.I.S associe le lamellé et le tissu en bambou, qui sont des dérivés modernes, avec des tiges de bambou. Aucun autre matériau ni colle ni vis ou autre n'a été ajouté. La conception des joints exploite au contraire les propriétés naturelles du bambou. Le tabouret (sans coussin) est constitué de sept éléments de trois types seulement, tous étant 100 % en bambou. La colle utilisée dans la fabrication du lamellé est biodégradable.

ESP

E.I.S (en castellano, "ejercicio de sencillez") es un taburete que obedece a dos reglas: la primera es que la confección sea lo más sencilla posible, minimizando los costes de producción, y la segunda, que esté hecha exclusivamente de bambú, un material que ofrece infinitas posibilidades gracias a su increíble fuerza, belleza, bajo coste y forma tubular natural. El E.I.S. combina el moderno laminado y la tela de bambú con las cañas naturales. No utiliza otros materiales, adhesivos ni clavos, dado que el diseño de las junturas aprovecha las características naturales del bambú. El taburete (sin cojín) consta de tres componentes con formas diferentes, un total de siete piezas, todas 100 % de bambú. La cola que se emplea en la producción del laminado también es biodegradable.

POR

E.I.S (Exercício em simplicidade) é um tamborete que segue duas regras: primeira, que se faça de forma tão simples quanto possível, mantendo assim custos mínimos de produção; e segunda, que se faça exclusivamente de bambu, um material imensamente versátil devido à sua incrível força, beleza, baixo custo, e forma tubular que ocorre de maneira natural. E.I.S. combina moderno laminado de bambu e tecido de bambu com tubos naturais de bambu. Não emprega nenhum outro material ou cola adicionada ou cravos. Em vez disso, o design das juntas explora as propriedades inatas do bambu. O tamborete (sem almofada) é feito de três componentes apenas, com formas diferentes, num total de sete peças, todas feitas 100 % de bambu. A cola usada na produção da laminagem também é biodegradável.

VITA, EQUUS
AND SERVUS

DESIGN FIRM
Florian Saul Design Development

DESIGNER
Florian Saul

PHOTOGRAPHY
Florian Saul

This table, stool, and clothes-rack set is manufactured using traditional bentwood techniques. The basic element of each piece is a closed frame of steam-bent oak. The characteristic curves and the slightly slanted straight lines are the unifying style elements. The particular appeal of the design lies in its simplicity, which stems from the reduction of parts and their minimized dimensioning. The use of sustainable materials such as wood and leather emphasizes the natural, handcrafted aesthetic.

GET UP
ESPARTO GRASS

DESIGN FIRM
Martín Azúa Studio

DESIGNER
Martín Azúa

PHOTOGRAPHY
Martín Azúa

Get Up is a furniture collection designed for resting and relaxing whose pieces lift up and stand freely when not in use, meaning they occupy less space. The Get Up collection is made from esparto, a type of grass found locally in Spain.

FRA

Get Up est une collection de meubles conçus pour le repos et la détente et qui se rangent debout pour occuper moins de place quand on ne les utilisent pas. La collection Get Up est faite en sparte, une graminée qui pousse en Espagne.

ESP

"Levántate" es una colección de muebles concebidos para el relax y el descanso, cuyos componentes se levantan y se sostienen solos cuando no se usan, lo que significa que ocupan menos espacio. La colección "Levántate" está hecha de esparto, una fibra que se obtiene de una planta típica de España.

POR

Te levanta é uma coleção de móveis concebidos para descansar e relaxar, cujas peças se levantam e se ficam em pé livremente quando não estão sendo usadas, o que significa que ocupam menos espaço. A coleção Te levanta é feita de esparto, um tipo de erva que se encontra localmente na Espanha.

EYRIE CHAIR

DESIGN FIRM
Studio Floris Wubben

DESIGNER
Floris Wubben

PHOTOGRAPHY
Floris Wubben

The bird's nest is an inventive piece of natural architecture. As a designer who works a lot with natural material, I have always been fascinated by these natural structures. The Eyrie Chair is an ode to these natural constructions. During my search for wooden branches I was specifically interested in their forms, which provided inspiration when making the design. Steam-bent ash has been used to make the nest. The joints between the ash slats are made from ash pins and wood glue. The frame has been constructed from wooden branches.

FRA

Le nid d'oiseau est un exemple inventif d'architecture naturelle. En tant que designer travaillant avec des matériaux naturels, j'ai toujours été fasciné par ces structures. La chaise Eyrie est un hommage à ces constructions naturelles. Lorsque je suis parti à la recherche de branches, j'ai surtout fait attention à leur forme qui m'a ensuite guidée pour élaborer les chaises. J'ai utilisé du frêne cintré pour fabriquer le « nid ». Les joints d'assemblage des lattes sont des chevilles en frêne également et de la colle à bois. Le socle est formé à partir de branches d'arbres.

ESP

Los nidos de los pájaros son una ingeniosa muestra de arquitectura en la naturaleza. Como diseñador que trabaja mucho con materiales naturales, siempre me han fascinado estas estructuras. La silla Eyrie es una oda a estas construcciones naturales. Cuando buscaba ramas de madera, me interesaban sobre todo sus formas, que inspiraron el diseño. He construido el nido con fresno moldeado al vapor. Las junturas que unen los listones están hechas de pernos de fresno y cola de madera. La estructura se basa en ramas de madera.

POR

O ninho de um pássaro é uma peça inventiva de arquitetura natural. Como designer que trabalha muito com materiais naturais, sempre estive fascinado por estas estruturas naturais. A cadeira Eyrie é uma ode a estas construções naturais. Durante minha procura de ramos de madeira, me interessava especialmente por suas formas, que proporcionaram inspiração ao realizar o design. Foi usado freixo dobrado a vapor para construir o ninho. As junções entre as ripas de freixo são feitas de parafusos de freixo e cola de madeira. A estrutura foi construída a partir de galhos de madeira.

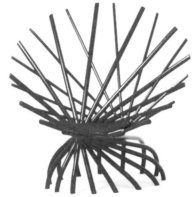

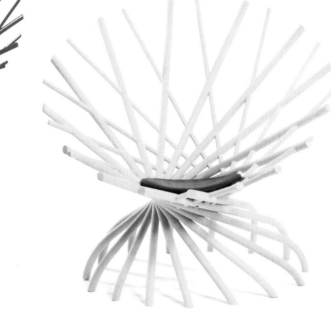

NEST

DESIGN FIRM
Markus Johansson Design Studio

DESIGNER
Markus Johansson

PHOTOGRAPHY
Markus Johansson

CLIENT
Markus Johansson Design Studio

Nest is created almost right out of the forest, letting nature challenge the straight, rigid, and traditional forms of modernist aestheticism. It's a nest for the home where one can relax in what might appear to be a swirling chaos of pegs. The chair offers a powerful illusion of movement and symmetry. Nest was the result of school project that began in 2010 and was finalized 2011. The chair is a free combination of round pegs without any "correct" angles, and is entirely made out of wood. Each of the thicker pegs is identical and each is cut at different lengths in order to facilitate the production process. Nest will become part of the permanent collection at MAD museum in New York in 2012.

FRA
Le fauteuil Nest semble sorti tout droit de la forêt, la nature prenant sa revanche sur les lignes droites et la raideur de l'esthétisme moderne. C'est un nid au creux duquel on peut se relaxer et qui a l'air d'un amas confus de branchages. De par sa conception, le fauteuil produit une illusion de mouvement et de symétrie. Nest est l'aboutissement d'un projet de recherche scolaire démarré en 2010 et terminé en 2011. Le fauteuil, entièrement en bois, est une combinaison libre de baguettes rondes sans aucune angularité. Toutes les baguettes de plus gros diamètre sont identiques. Elles sont sciées suivant différentes longueurs pour faciliter le processus de production. Nest fera bientôt partie de la collection permanente du musée MAD de New York en 2012.

ESP
Este nido está sacado del bosque, para que la naturaleza desafíe las formas tradicionales, inflexibles y estrictas del esteticismo modernista. Se trata de un nido doméstico en el que podemos relajarnos en medio de un aparente caos de barras de madera. La silla ofrece una poderosa ilusión de movimiento y simetría. Nido es el resultado de un proyecto académico que se desarrolla entre 2010 y 2011. La silla es una combinación libre de barras redondas en la que no se observa ningún ángulo "correcto" y está completamente hecha de madera. Las más gruesas son idénticas y están cortadas en trechos desiguales con el fin de facilitar el proceso de producción. Nido forma parte de la colección permanente del museo MAD de Nueva York desde 2012.

POR
Ninho foi criado quase à beira do bosque, permitindo que a natureza desafie as formas tradicionais retas e rígidas do esteticismo modernista. É um ninho para a casa onde a pessoa pode relaxar em algo que poderia parecer um caos revolto de varetas de madeira. A cadeira oferece um poderoso efeito ilusório de movimento e simetria. Ninho foi o resultado de um projeto de escola que começou em 2010 e acabou em 2011. A cadeira é uma combinação livre de varetas redondas sem nenhum ângulo "correto", e está totalmente confeccionada em madeira. Cada uma das varetas mais grossas é idêntica e está cortada em diferentes comprimentos para facilitar o processo de produção. Ninho será parte da coleção permanente do museu MAD de Nova York em 2012.

ELDA CHAIR

DESIGN FIRM
Scoope Design

PHOTOGRAPHY
citylifephotography.com

DESIGNERS
Elda Bellone & Davide Carbone

Elda is a versatile and dynamic piece of furniture with a playful component of functionality that brings a breath of fresh air to the conventional connotations of a simple domestic object. It's a fun, versatile accessory which, usefully for when it is in ladder mode, is also scratch resistant. Elda was designed and manufactured exclusively using sustainable materials, from its wooden structure to the water-based paint finish, the 100 percent woolen-felt hood, and the magnetic locking system that holds it in position. Everything has been designed with a focus on sustainability and leaving no footprint.

FRA
Elda est une chaise-escabeau. Elda est un meuble polyvalent et dynamique, dont la double fonctionnalité apporte une touche d'originalité et de fantaisie dans le monde banal des objets à usage domestique. C'est un accessoire pratique et amusant qui résiste en plus aux rayures lorsqu'il est en mode escabeau. La chaise-escabeau Elda a été conçue et fabriquée en matériaux durables, allant de sa structure en bois, à la peinture à l'eau, en passant par son dossier en feutre pure laine et le système à aimant qui le verrouille en position. Tout a été conçu dans une optique de durabilité et d'empreinte écologique minime.

ESP
Elda es un mueble versátil y dinámico, con un componente lúdico y funcional que insufla un soplo de aire fresco a las connotaciones convencionales de un sencillo objeto doméstico. Se trata de un accesorio adaptable y divertido que no raya las superficies cuando se utiliza como escalera. Elda está diseñada y fabricada exclusivamente con materiales sostenibles; desde la estructura de madera hasta el acabado de pintura con base de agua, la funda 100 % de fieltro de algodón y el sistema de cierre magnético que la sujeta, todo se ha diseñado de forma que sea sostenible y no deje ninguna huella.

POR
Elda é um móvel versátil e dinâmico, com um componente alegre de funcionalidade que traz um ar fresco às conotações convencionais de um simples objeto doméstico. É um acessório divertido e versátil, útil quando está no modo escada e também é resistente a riscos. Elda foi projetada e fabricada usando-se, exclusivamente, materiais sustentáveis, desde a sua estrutura de madeira até ao acabamento de pintura baseada em água, o capuz 100 % de feltro de algodão e o sistema de fecho magnético que a fixa em sua posição. Tudo foi projetado com foco na sustentabilidade e sem deixar pegada.

ZIGGY AND ZAGGY

DESIGN FIRM
Frankie

DESIGNER
Frank Neulichedl

Ziggy is a table chair who in spite of being only eight inches tall packs in a lot of design. The trapezoid design combined with sharply pointed lines give him a dynamic feel that makes other seats go green with envy. Zaggy acts a little shy, but it's just because of his knockknees, which are exactly what give him his character and make him irresistibly charming. His design gives him lightness, elegance, and a robust functionality. Both Ziggy and Zaggy are made from naturally waxed beech that comes from sustainable sources and ecological glue; both are completely metal free.

FRA
Ziggy est une chaise, qui avec ses 20 cm de haut, est un concentré de design. Le dessin trapézoïdal combiné aux angles aigus lui confèrent un indéniable dynamisme. Quant à la table Zaggy, elle est plus discrète avec ses « genoux pointus », et c'est ce qui fait son charme. À la fois légère, élégante et robuste. Ziggy et Zaggy sont faits en bouleau ciré provenant de sources durables et de colle écologique, et ne contiennent aucun élément en métal.

ESP
Ziggy es una silla de mesa que, aunque solo mide 20 centímetros de alto, encierra mucho diseño. El diseño trapezoide, en combinación con las líneas afiladas, le insufla una sensación de dinamismo. Zaggy es algo tímido, pero solo porque tiene las rodillas torcidas, aunque eso es exactamente lo que le da carácter y lo hace irresistiblemente atractivo. El diseño es liviano, elegante y decididamente funcional. Ziggy y Zaggy están hechos con haya naturalmente encerada de origen sostenible y cola ecológica; ninguno de ellos tiene componentes metálicos.

POR
Ziggy é uma cadeira de mesa que apesar de ter só de oito polegadas de altura introduz muito design. O design trapezoide combinado com linhas de pontas agudas lhe dão uma sensação dinâmica que faz com que outros assentos fiquem verdes de inveja. Zaggy atua com certa timidez, mas isto só se deve aos seus joelhos abatidos, que são exatamente o que lhe confere caráter e a convertem em irresistivelmente atraente. Seu design lhe dá leveza, elegância e uma funcionalidade sólida. Tanto Ziggy como Zaggy são feitas de faia naturalmente encerada de origem sustentável e cola ecológica; ambas estão totalmente isentas de metal.

DE TAFELWIP / THE CURTESSY TABLE

DESIGN FIRM
Marleen Jansen Product Design

DESIGNER
Marleen Jansen

PHOTOGRAPHY
Wim de Leeuw

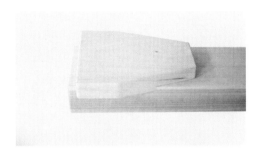

This project is an interactive art object that subjects its users to the challenging balancing act of getting their table manners right. It was developed from Marleen Jansen's dissertation on the subject of table manners, entitled "Being Forced Voluntarily." To resolve the issue of how to prevent people from walking away from the table while having dinner, Marleen created this table with see-saw seating. If one person leaves the table, the other diner ends up on the floor.

FRA
Ce projet est un objet d'art interactif qui met au défi ses utilisateurs de se balancer sans rien perdre de leurs bonnes manières. La table a été inspirée par la thèse de doctorat de Marleen Jansen sur l'art de bien se tenir à table et intitulée « Volontairement forcés ». Pour résoudre le problème des gens qui se lèvent de table au cours d'un repas, Marleen a créé ce système dont les sièges sont une balançoire à bascule. Lorsqu'un convive se lève, l'autre se retrouve par terre.

ESP
Este proyecto es un objeto de arte interactivo que somete a los usuarios al difícil desafío de mantener las formas en la mesa. Se basa en la tesis de Marleen Jansen sobre los modales en la mesa titulada "La obligación voluntaria". Para que los comensales no se levanten de la mesa durante la comida, Marleen ha diseñado esta mesa con asiento en forma de balancín, de manera que si uno de los comensales se levanta de la mesa, el otro acaba en el suelo.

POR
Este projeto é um objeto de arte interativo que desafia seus usuários ao ato balanceado de ter boas maneiras em mesa. Foi desenvolvido a partir da dissertação de Marleem Jansem sobre o assunto de maneiras em mesa, intitulado "Ser forçado voluntariamente". Para resolver a questão de como evitar que as pessoas se levantam da mesa enquanto estão comendo, Marleem criou esta mesa com um assento gangorra. Se uma pessoa se levanta da mesa, o outro comensal acaba no chão.

STUMP AND TRUNK

DESIGN FIRM
Kalon Studios

DESIGNERS
Johannes Pauwen & Michaele Simmering

CLIENT
Kalon Studios.

Stump was inspired by the original stool: a tree stump. Raw and unfinished, Stump and Trunk celebrate the natural qualities of the tree trunk. FSC-certified maple and ash are both indigenous to North America, and both are also a familiar feature in Kalon Studios' products. Stump and Trunk are cut from the green wood of a tree trunk so the surface splits as it ages and dries, giving each piece a unique look. These trunks mostly come from storm-damaged trees.

FRA

La source d'inspiration de Stump est le premier tabouret de l'histoire, à savoir la souche d'un arbre. Fabriqués en bois brut, Stump and Trunk rendent hommage au tronc d'arbre. L'érable et le frêne, tous deux FSC et originaires d'Amérique du nord, font partie des matériaux préférés de Kalon Studios. Stump and Trunk sont découpés dans le tronc d'un arbre vert pour que le bois se fende à mesure qu'il sèche et vieillit et confère à chaque meuble sa propre personnalité. La plupart des troncs proviennent d'arbres tombés lors de tempêtes.

POR

Toco inspirou-se no tamborete original: um toco de árvore. Em bruto e sem acabar, Toco e tronco ostentam as qualidades naturais do tronco de árvore. Plátano e freixo com certificado FSC são próprios da América do Norte e ambos são característica familiar nos produtos de Kalon Studios. Toco e tronco estão cortados da madeira verde de um tronco de árvore, de forma que a superfície se racha ao envelhecer e secar, dando uma aparência única a cada peça. A maioria destes troncos é proveniente de árvores danificadas por tormentas.

ESP

El tocón se inspira en el taburete más antiguo: un tocón de árbol. Inconclusos y toscos, el tocón y el tronco celebran las cualidades naturales de los troncos de los árboles. El arce y el fresno, ambos con certificado del FSC, son de origen norteamericano y ambos son materiales habituales en los productos de Kalon Studios. El tocón y el tronco están tallados con la madera verde de un tronco, de manera que la superficie se resquebraja cuando envejece y se seca, lo que le confiere una apariencia única a cada pieza. La mayoría son troncos de árboles que han sufrido daños a causa de las tormentas.

SHAVINGS

DESIGNER
Yoav Avinoam

PHOTOGRAPHY
Bezalel

Using waste sawdust from the wood industry is a response to the way we view our usage and exploitation of materials in modern culture. The sawdust, which comes from different kinds of wood, is pressed with resin into a mold that also contains the other parts of the furniture. This method provides an opportunity to explorenew ways of combiningthe legs of the furniture and the sawdust. Alongside the way in which the sawdust crumbles toward the edges, this method also creates a new aesthetic for a material once destined to be waste.

FRA

Nous avons décidé d'utiliser la sciure rejetée par l'industrie du bois pour attirer l'attention sur l'usage et l'exploitation des matériaux dans notre culture moderne. La sciure, qui provient de différents types de bois, est pressée avec de la résine dans un moule qui contient également les autres éléments du meuble. Cette méthode nous permet d'explorer de nouvelles façons de combiner les pieds du meuble et la sciure en jouant sur les joints d'assemblage. En modulant sa répartition au niveau des pieds, cette méthode produit une nouvelle esthétique à partir d'un matériau qui était destiné au rebut.

ESP

El uso del serrín sobrante de la industria maderera es una reacción frente a nuestra visión del uso y la explotación de los materiales en la cultura moderna. El serrín, que se obtiene de diversos tipos de madera, se prensa junto con la resina en un molde que también contiene las demás partes del mueble. Gracias a este método se exploran nuevas combinaciones del serrín y las patas de los muebles. Asi como los bordes del serrín se desmigajan, este método crea una nueva estética para una materia que estaba destinada a convertirse en basura.

POR

Usar os resíduos de serragem da indústria madeireira é uma resposta à maneira com que observamos nosso uso e exploração de materiais na cultura moderna. A serragem, proveniente de diferentes tipos de madeira, é prensada com resina num molde que também contém outras partes do móvel. Este método proporciona uma oportunidade de explorar novas vias de combinar as pernas dos móveis e a serragem. Pelo modo como a serragem se esmigalha nas bordas, este método cria também uma nova estética para um material destinado a ser lixo.

FRA

TECHNOLOGIE ET ARTISANAT

Les magnifiques créations présentées dans ce chapitre. Les meubles associent créativité, écologie, artisanat et haute technologie pour notre plus grand bonheur.

Les meubles décrits dans ce chapitre tirent parti de différents types de technologies et matériaux modernes, comme la fibre de carbone, le papier-ciment, le film polyuréthane, le nylon rempli de verre et les techniques de rotomoulage, ainsi que de nouveaux matériaux et concepts écologiques mis au point par les designers eux-mêmes.

POR

TECNOLOGIA E ARTES

Os maravilhosos trabalhos incluídos neste capítulo demonstram quão criativo e ecológico pode ser o mobiliário que incorpora elementos de alta tecnologia ou tecnologias únicas de fabricação.

As peças de mobiliário aqui apresentadas utilizam diferentes tipos de tecnologia e materiais contemporâneos, como fibra de carbono, concreto de papel, camada de nanômetro, camada de poliuretano, nylon enchimento de vidro e técnicas de moldagem rotativa, assim como novos materiais eco e conceitos eco desenvolvidos pelos próprios designers.

ESP

TECNOLOGÍA Y ARTESANÍA

Las maravillosas obras que se incluyen en este capítulo demuestran que los muebles que utilizan elementos tecnológicos o técnicas de fabricación únicas también son creativos y ecológicos.

Los muebles que ahora le presentamos emplean diferentes tipos de tecnología y materiales contemporáneos, como la fibra de carbono, el hormigón de papel, las películas de nanometría y poliuretano, el nailon relleno de vidrio y las técnicas de moldeado rotativo, así como los nuevos materiales y conceptos ecológicos que desarrollan los propios diseñadores.

03
102-141

TECHNOLOGY & CRAFTS

The wonderful works included in this chapter demonstrate just how creative and ecological furniture that incorporates high-tech elements or unique manufacturing technologies can be.

The pieces of furniture featured here make use of different types of contemporary technology and materials, such as carbon fiber, paper crete, nanometer film, polyurethane film, glass-filled nylon, and roto molding techniques, as well as new eco materials and eco concepts developed by the designers themselves.

CABBAGE CHAIR

DESIGN FIRM
Nendo

DESIGNER
Oki Sato

PHOTOGRAPHY
Masayuki Hayashi

CLIENT
XXIst Century Man Exhibition

Nendo designed the Cabbage Chair for the *XXIst Century Man* exhibition, curated by Issey Miyake, to commemorate the first anniversary of 21_21 Design Sight in Roppongi, Tokyo. Resins that are added during the original paper production process add strength and the ability to fix the forms, while the pleats give the chair elasticity and a springy resilience, for an overall effect that looks almost rough, but gives the user a soft, comfortable seating experience. The chair has no internal structure. It is not finished, and it is assembled without nails or screws. This primitive design is a gentle response to fabrication and distribution costs and environmental concerns that we face in the twenty-first century.

ESP
Nendo diseñó la silla repollo para la exposición *XXIst Century Man* de Issey Miyake, que conmemoraba el primer aniversario de 21_21 Design Sight en Roppongi, Tokio. Las resinas que se añaden durante la producción del papel fortalecen y asientan las formas; asimismo, gracias a los pliegues la silla es elástica, resistente y esponjosa, de manera que el efecto resultante es casi áspero, aunque de hecho el usuario disfruta de una experiencia mullida y confortable. La silla carece de estructura interna. No está terminada y no hacen falta clavos ni pernos para montarla. Este diseño primitivo es una respuesta amable a los costes de fabricación y distribución y las cuestiones medioambientales a las que nos enfrentamos en el siglo XXI.

FRA
Nendo a créé le pouf Cabbage Chair pour l'exposition *XXIst Century Man*, dont Issey Miyake était le commissaire, qui commémorait le premier anniversaire de 21_21 Design Sight à Roppongi, Tokyo. Les résines qui sont ajoutées au cours du processus de fabrication du papier lui confèrent une plus grande résistance et malléabilité. Grâce aux plis, le pouf est souple tout en résistant à l'écrasement. Extérieurement, le pouf peut sembler un peu raide, mais il est au contraire moelleux et particulièrement confortable. Il est dépourvu de structure interne et ne possède aucun revêtement. Il est assemblé sans clous ni vis. Le dessin basique est une manière de limiter les coûts de fabrication et de distribution et de relever les défis environnementaux du XXIe siècle.

POR
Nendo desenhou a Cadeira repolho para a exposição *XXIst Century Man*, organizada por Issey Miyake, para comemorar o primeiro aniversário de 21_21 Design Sight em Roppongi, Tóquio. As resinas que se adicionam durante o processo original de produção de papel adicionam força e a capacidade de fixar as formas, enquanto as dobras dão à cadeira elasticidade e resiliência fofa, para um efeito total que parece quase áspero, mas proporciona ao usuário uma experiência de assento suave e cômodo. A cadeira não tem estrutura interna. Não está acabada, e se monta sem pregos ou parafusos. Este design primitivo é uma resposta amável aos custos de fabricação e distribuição e preocupações ambientais com as quais nos defrontamos no século vinte e um.

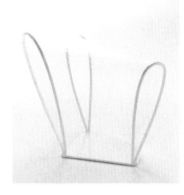

TRANSPARENT CHAIR

DESIGN FIRM
Nendo

DESIGNER
Oki Sato

PHOTOGRAPHY
Masayuki Hayashi

This chair is made with transparent polyurethane film, which is commonly used as a packing material for precision instruments and products that are susceptible to vibrations and shock due to its high elasticity and ability to return to its original state. Looking at the chair, it seems to consist of nothing but a backrest and armrests. It wraps around the body and supports it like a hammock, providing a light, floating feeling for the sitter.

FRA
Cette chaise est fabriquée avec du film de polyuréthane transparent que l'on utilise couramment pour emballer les instruments de précision et les produits sensibles aux vibrations et aux chocs, car c'est une matière très élastique capable de reprendre sa forme initiale. Au prime abord, la chaise a l'air d'être composée uniquement d'un dossier et de deux accoudoirs. Le film transparent tendu entre ces trois éléments épouse parfaitement la forme du corps et le soutient à la manière d'un hamac. La personne qui s'y assoit a l'impression de flotter légèrement.

ESP
Esta silla está hecha con una película transparente de poliuretano, que suele emplearse como embalaje de instrumentos de precisión y artículos sensibles a las vibraciones y los golpes, dado que es muy elástica y recupera la forma. A primera vista, diríamos que la silla se compone solamente de respaldo y reposabrazos, aunque de hecho envuelve el cuerpo del usuario y lo sostiene a la manera de una hamaca, al tiempo que le transmite una sensación de ingravidez.

POR
Esta cadeira é feita de uma camada transparente de poliuretano, que normalmente se usa como material de embalagem para instrumentos de precisão e produtos que são suscetíveis às vibrações e batimentos, devido à sua grande elasticidade e capacidade para voltar ao estado original. Olhando à cadeira, parece que é composta apenas pelo apoio e o apoio de braços. Envolve o corpo e o prende como uma rede, proporcionando uma sensação leve e flutuante a quem nela se senta.

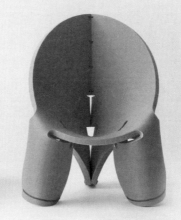
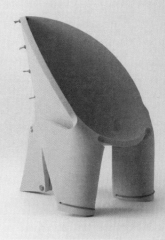

EVA CHAIR FOR KIDS

DESIGN FIRM
h220430

PHOTOGRAPHY
Ikunori Yamamoto

The EVA Chair has been designed for just such children. It is assembled simply by rolling a piece of board and fastening it with a string. Because it can be turned into a flat shape easily, it can be stored in small spaces and is also efficient to ship in terms of costs and energy usage. The material used to make the EVA Chair is lightweight and highly flexible, with a superior durability and various color options. The material does not present a risk if it accidentally enters into a child's mouth, making it a good material for children. In an age where the priorities are for materials to be highly recyclable, dioxin free, and environmentally friendly, the material used to make the EVA Chair is a suitable one for the children who will play an important role in the future.

FRA
La chaise EVA a été conçue pour ces enfants-là. Pour la monter, il suffit de dérouler une plaque et de l'attacher avec une ficelle. Et comme on peut la mettre à plat en un tournemain, elle peut se ranger dans un petit espace et être expédiée à peu de frais, en termes de coûts et de consommation d'énergie. Le matériau utilisé pour la fabrication de la chaise EVA est léger, extrêmement souple, très résistant et existe en différentes couleurs. Par ailleurs, il ne présente aucun danger si l'enfant le porte à la bouche, ce qui en fait une matière de choix pour les tout-petits. À une époque où l'on privilégie l'utilisation de matériaux recyclables, écologiques et sans dioxine, la chaise EVA est tout à fait dans l'air du temps et parfaitement adaptée aux enfants qui auront un rôle important à jouer dans le futur.

ESP
La silla EVA está diseñada para ellos. Se monta enrollando una plancha y sujetándola con una cuerda. Como se estira fácilmente, puede guardarse en espacios reducidos y despacharse con el mínimo coste y consumo de energía. Está hecha de un material ligero, flexible y duradero que además se presenta en diversos colores y no entraña ningún riesgo si el niño se lo mete en la boca accidentalmente, de modo que es idóneo para los diseños infantiles. En una época en la que los materiales deben ser reciclables, desprovistos de dioxinas y respetuosos con el medioambiente, la silla EVA es perfecta para los niños que desempeñarán una función importante en el futuro.

POR
A cadeira EVA foi desenhada para estas crianças. É montada simplesmente enrolando uma placa e fixando a mesma com uma corda. Como é possível voltar a deixá-la plana com facilidade, pode ser guardada em espaços pequenos e também é eficaz para transportar em termos de custos e uso de energia. O material usado para fazer a cadeira EVA é leve e altamente flexível, com uma durabilidade superior e com várias opções de cor. O material não apresenta perigo se entrar na boca de uma criança acidentalmente, o que o torna um bom material para crianças. Numa era em que as prioridades são os materiais altamente recicláveis, sem dioxinas e favoráveis ao meio ambiente, o material usado para fazer a cadeira EVA é adequado para as crianças que desempenharão um papel importante no futuro.

IVY CHAIR

DESIGN FIRM
h220430

Living in cities where nature is almost completely excluded, we tend to forget that we depend on the power of nature and only remember it when natural disaster strikes. However, we believe that it is essential that we appreciate nature and always respect it. The white but otherwise realistic leaves of the Ivy Chair act as a metaphor for the exclusion of nature from the city. The artificial white color of the Ivy Chair merges it into daily life without presenting a sense of incompatibility. The intention of the Ivy Chair is to make you feel comfortable, as if you were surrounded by trees and flowers. Whenever you sit down in the chair it will prompt you to think about nature above its function as a chair.

FRA

À force de vivre dans un environnement dont la nature est pratiquement exclue, on finit par oublier que l'on dépend entièrement d'elle. Il suffit d'une catastrophe naturelle pour être rappelés brutalement à l'ordre. Nous pensons qu'il est important de reconnaître ce que la nature nous donne et de toujours la respecter. Les feuilles du fauteuil Ivy qui, hormis la couleur blanche artificielle, sont très réalistes, symbolisent la nature absente de nos villes. C'est cette couleur, justement, qui permet au lierre de s'intégrer harmonieusement à notre quotidien. Le fauteuil Ivy a pour mission de vous accueillir confortablement, comme si vous étiez environné d'arbres et de fleurs. Chaque fois que vous prendrez place dans le fauteuil Ivy, vous penserez à la nature plutôt qu'à sa fonction de siège.

ESP

Cuando vivimos en ciudades en las que la naturaleza se encuentra casi completamente ausente, con frecuencia olvidamos que dependemos del poder de la naturaleza y solo nos acordamos de ella cuando acontecen catástrofes naturales. Sin embargo, nosotros creemos que debemos amarla y respetarla en todo momento. Las hojas blancas, aunque realistas, de la silla de hiedra son una metáfora de la exclusión de la naturaleza en las ciudades. El color blanco artificial de la silla de hiedra la introduce en la vida cotidiana sin que resulte incompatible. La intención es que se sienta cómodo, como si estuviera rodeado de árboles y flores. Siempre que se siente, hará que piense en la naturaleza, más allá de la función que desempeña como silla.

POR

Vivendo nas cidades onde a natureza está quase totalmente excluída, tendemos a esquecer de que dependemos do poder da natureza e só nos lembramos disso quando ocorre um desastre natural. No entanto, cremos que é essencial que apreciemos a natureza e a respeitemos sempre. As folhas brancas, mas simultaneamente realistas, da Cadeira de hera atuam como metáfora para a exclusão da natureza da cidade. A cor branca artificial da Cadeira de hera mistura-a na vida diária sem dar uma sensação de incompatibilidade. A intenção da Cadeira de hera é fazer com que você se sinta confortável, como se estivesse rodeado de árvores e flores. Sempre que você se sentar na cadeira, ela lhe fará pensar na natureza, excedendo a sua função como cadeira.

HUT-HUT

DESIGN FIRM
Kalon Studios

CLIENT
Kalon Studios

DESIGNERS
Johannes Pauwen & Michaele Simmering

Hut-Hut is a playful reinterpretation of the rocking horse. Made from solid blocks of FSC-certified wood on a five-axis CNC machine, the engraved star pattern is both a decorative element and an efficient use of machining time. Rather than resurfacing the piece to hide the machining lines, they have been incorporated into the piece as a decorative element, reducing the surface's machining time by 75 percent. Hut-Hut Kids, meanwhile, is cast from brightly-colored, sustainable resin that is 100 percent recycled from postindustrial materials. Hut-Hut pieces are CNC milled and hand finished. CNC-Milling is a highly efficient form of manufacturing, maximizing time, labor, and material efficiency. Product development was carried out using computer and image files, thus cutting down on the use of raw materials. Hut-Hut resin pieces are machine cast and rotomolded to order, one at a time.

FRA
Hut-Hut est une réinterprétation du cheval à bascule. Fabriqué à partir de blocs en bois massif certifié FSC sur une machine cinq axes à commandes numériques, le motif central en forme d'étoile n'est pas juste une décoration : c'est le résultat d'une utilisation efficace du temps machine. Au lieu de poncer la pièce pour faire disparaître les traits d'usinage, ceux-ci ont été délibérément conservés à titre d'éléments décoratifs, le temps passé à fabriquer la pièce ayant été réduit de 75 %. La version pour enfants du siège, Hut-Hut Kids, est moulée dans une résine durable recyclée à 100 % à partir de matériaux postindustriels. Les sièges Hut-Hut sont usinés sur une machine à commandes numériques et finis à la main. L'usinage numérique est une méthode de fabrication hautement efficace qui exploite au mieux le temps, la main d'œuvre et le matériau. Le produit a été mis au point par ordinateur de manière à réduire la quantité de matériaux bruts nécessaires. Les sièges Hut-Hut en résine sont fondus et rotomoulés à la demande, un par un, pour éviter les invendus, et donc le gâchis.

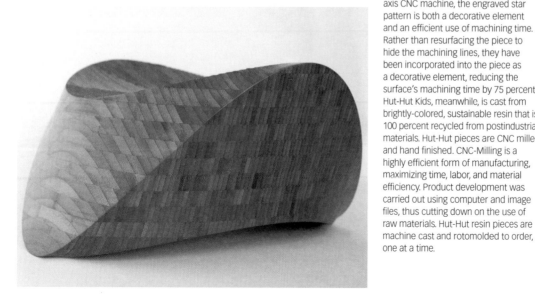

ESP

Hut-Hut es una reinterpretación lúdica del caballito de madera hecha con bloques de madera con certificado del FSC en una fresadora CNC de cinco ejes. La estrella grabada es un elemento decorativo al tiempo que un ejemplo de un uso eficiente del tiempo de producción; en lugar de ocultar estas líneas, se han incorporado como elemento decorativo, disminuyendo el tiempo de trabajo en la superficie en un 75 %. Por su parte, Hut-Hut Kids está teñido con resina sostenible de colores brillantes, 100% reciclada de materiales posindustriales. Los componentes de Hut-Hut están horadados con una fresadora CNC y acabados a mano. El fresado CNC es muy eficiente y maximiza el tiempo, el trabajo y el rendimiento de los materiales. El desarrollo del producto se basa en imágenes y archivos informáticos, disminuyendo el uso de materias primas. Las resinas de Hut-Hut se pintan a máquina y se rotomoldean de una en una a petición del cliente.

POR

Hut-Hut é uma reinterpretação alegre do cavalo agitador. Feito de blocos sólidos de madeira certificada FSC com uma máquina CNC de cinco eixos, o desenho da estrela gravada é tanto um elemento decorativo como um uso eficaz do tempo de usinagem. Em lugar de revestir a peça para esconder as linhas de usinagem, estas foram incorporadas na peça como elemento decorativo, reduzindo o tempo de usinagem da superfície em 75 %. Hut-Hut Kids, e que é tingido com resina sustentável de cores brilhantes, 100 % reciclada de materiais pós-industriais. As peças Hut-Hut são usinadas com CNC e acabadas à mão. A usinagem com CNC é uma forma altamente eficaz de fabricar, que maximiza o tempo, o trabalho e a eficiência do material. O desenvolvimento do produto foi feito usando computador e arquivos de imagem, diminuindo assim o uso de matérias-primas. As peças de resina Hut-Hut são pintadas a máquina e se moldam por rotação e sob encomenda, uma a uma.

PANE CHAIR

DESIGN FIRM
Tokujin Yoshioka Inc.

DESIGNER
Tokujin Yoshioka

PHOTOGRAPHY
Nacasa & Partners Inc.

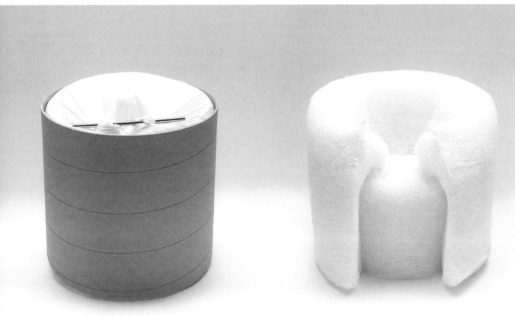

Going against conventional wisdom, his idea for a future structure was not to achieve strength using hard materials, but to systematically organize small fibers so as to gain more strength by spreading the stress. Tokujin wondered if he could create an entirely new type of chair that feels like sitting on air and in which the fiber itself is the structural body. After a good deal of trial and error, he came up with a chair whose finish is uncertain until it has been baked in a kiln. He named it after a type of food that everybody in the world is familiar with: the PANE (Italian for bread) chair. The PANE Chair goes through almost the same steps as baking bread. A semi-cylindrical block of fibers is rolled and inserted into a paper tube, and as it is baked in a kiln at 104 degrees centigrade the fibers memorize the shape of the chair. It is way beyond the conventional methods of making a chair; it is a bread-like chair.

FRA

Au lieu de suivre les conventions préconisant l'usage de matériaux durs pour créer des objets solides, il imagina une structure formée de fibres fines organisées de manière à répartir la charge pour gagner en résistance. Tokujin s'est demandé s'il pouvait réellement créer un nouveau type de siège qui donnerait l'impression de s'assoire sur de l'air, et dont la structure même serait en fibres. Après de nombreux tâtonnements, il a fini par créer un fauteuil qui doit être passé au four lors de l'étape finale. C'est pourquoi il l'a appelé PANE, qui signifie « pain » en italien et qui est un aliment que tout le monde connaît. Au cours de son élaboration, le fauteuil PANE passe pratiquement par les mêmes étapes que le pain. On forme un boudin à partir d'un bloc de fibres semi-cylindrique que l'on l'enfile dans un manchon en papier. On le met au four et on le cuit à 104° Celsius, opération au cours de laquelle le fauteuil va mémoriser sa forme. C'est complètement différent de la manière habituelle de fabriquer un fauteuil ! C'est comme si on faisait un fauteuil en pâte à pain.

ESP

En contra de la creencia popular, la fuerza de esta estructura futura no se basa en el uso de materiales duros, sino en la organización sistemática de las fibras pequeñas para distribuir la presión. Tokujin se preguntó si podría crear una silla completamente nueva que diera la sensación de que el usuario se sentaba en el aire, en la que la propia fibra fuera la estructura. Después de un buen número de ensayos y errores, ideó una silla en la que el acabado es una incógnita hasta que se cuece en un horno y le puso el nombre de un alimento que conoce todo el mundo: PAN. La silla PAN sigue casi los mismos pasos que el pan horneado. Se enrolla un bloque semicilíndrico de fibras, se inserta en un tubo de papel y se cuece en un horno a 104 °C mientras las fibras memorizan la forma. Va más allá de los métodos convencionales; es una silla semejante a un pan.

POR

Contra a sabedoria convencional, sua ideia de uma estrutura futura não era conseguir força usando materiais duros, mas sim organizar sistematicamente pequenas fibras para ganhar mais força ao distribuir a pressão. Tokujin se perguntava se poderia criar um tipo de cadeira totalmente novo que fizesse uma pessoa sentir-se no ar e na qual a própria fibra fosse o corpo estrutural. Depois de uma boa quantidade de tentativa e erro, descobriu uma cadeira cujo acabamento era inseguro até que se cozinhasse num forno. Deu-lhe o nome de um tipo de comida com a qual todo o mundo está familiarizado: a cadeira PÃO. A cadeira PÃO passa quase que pelos mesmos passos que o pão estufado. Um bloco semicilíndrico de fibras se enrola e se insere num tubo de papel, e enquanto se cozinha num forno a 104 °C, as fibras memorizam a forma da cadeira. Ultrapassa os métodos convencionais de se fazer uma cadeira; é uma cadeira tipo pão.

FLUX CHAIR

DESIGN FIRM
Flux Furniture

DESIGNERS
Douwe Jacobs & Tom Schouten

PHOTOGRAPHY
Eelke Dekker

At Flux they like designer furniture. They also like things that are simple, sustainable, and flexible. So when they began designing Flux Furniture, they kept all this in mind. Flux are also all about folding. Their award-winning chairs are made from one craftily cut piece of sustainable polypropylene and are engineered to be assembled without the use of any tools. Flux think this folding business is quite clever; it means that their chairs look the way they look because they work the way they work. Their goal is to create an entire range of simple, sustainable designs. They will probably involve folding...

FRA
Chez Flux, ils aiment les meubles design. Ils apprécient aussi les choses simples, durables et souples. Ils ont ainsi bien tenu compte de ces trois critères lorsqu'ils ont mis au point la chaise Flux. Flux a aussi une autre qualité : elle est pliante. Ce siège ingénieux qui a gagné de nombreux prix, est fabriqué dans une seule pièce de polypropylène durable et est conçue pour être montée sans avoir besoin d'outils. Chez Flux, ils savent qu'ils ont raison de travailler comme ils le font, ils ont pris le pli ! Leur objectif est de développer une gamme complète de designs simples et durables. Ça ne va pas faire un pli, c'est sûr !

ESP
En Flux les gustan los muebles de diseño y las cosas sencillas, sostenibles y flexibles, de manera que cuando diseñaron el Mobiliario Flux tuvieron todo esto en cuenta. Flux también se basa en los pliegues. Sus galardonadas sillas están hechas de una plancha de polipropileno sostenible que se corta mediante métodos artesanales y se montan sin una sola herramienta. En Flux consideran que los pliegues son muy ingeniosos; gracias a ellos, sus sillas tienen el aspecto que tienen porque funcionan como funcionan. Su objetivo es crear una gama completa de diseños sencillos y sostenibles. Seguramente estarán basadas en pliegues...

POR
Na Flux ,gostam do mobiliário de designer. E também gostam das coisas simples, sustentáveis e flexíveis. Deste modo, quando começaram a criar o Mobiliário de Flux, tiveram tudo isto em conta. Flux também é dobrar. Suas cadeiras vencedoras de prêmios são feitas de uma só peça artesanalmente cortada de polipropileno sustentável e são construídas para serem montadas sem usar nem sequer uma ferramenta. Na Flux pensam que essa coisa de dobrar é bastante inteligente; significa que suas cadeiras parecem o que parecem porque funcionam como funcionam. Seu objetivo é criar uma gama completa de design simples e sustentáveis. Provavelmente envolverão dobragem...

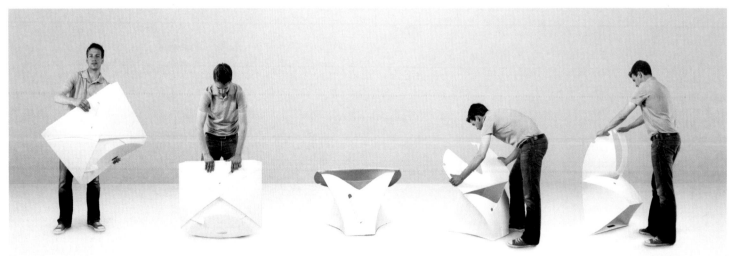

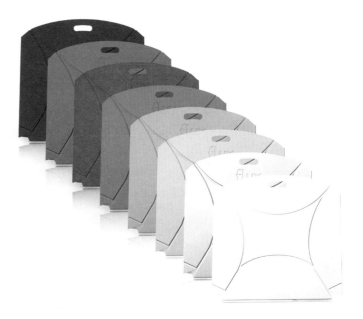

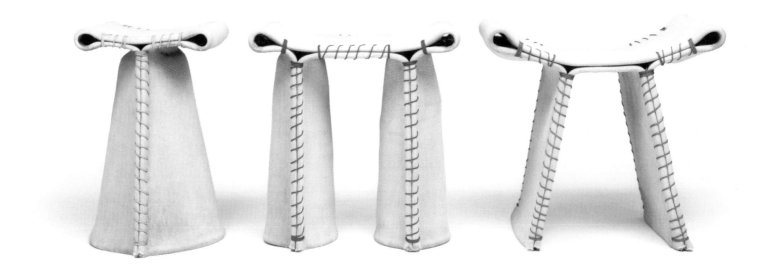

STITCHING CONCRETE

DESIGN FIRM
Florian Schmid

DESIGNER
Florian Schmid

PHOTOGRAPHY
Florian Schmid

Stitching Concrete is a project inspired by the contrasts of the material Concrete Canvas. These stools are made by folding Concrete Canvas, a fabric that has been impregnated with a layer of cement and has a PVC backing, and then drenching it in water. Once soaked, it can be manipulated for a few hours before hardening. A wooden mold supports it while it dries over a period of twenty-four hours. Before it dries the edges are stitched together with brightly colored thread. The material combines the warm softness of the cloth and the stability of the cold concrete, while the finished surface keeps its soft appearance.

FRA
Le projet Stitching Concrete tire son inspiration de la fusion entre le béton et la couture. Le matériau utilisé est le Concrete Canvas, un tissu imprégné d'une couche de ciment et doté d'un renfort en PVC que l'on trempe dans l'eau. Une fois mouillée, cette matière devient malléable et peut se travailler pendant quelques heures avant qu'elle ne sèche. La pièce façonnée est placée sur un moule en bois pour le séchage qui dure 24 heures. Juste avant qu'elle ne soit complètement sèche, ses bords sont cousus avec du fil de couleur vive. Le matériau combine le moelleux du tissu et la stabilité du béton froid, la surface lisse renforçant la douceur de son aspect.

ESP
El proyecto hormigón cosido se inspira en los contrastes de la lona de hormigón. Estos taburetes se fabrican doblando lonas de hormigón, una tela impregnada con una capa de cemento y un sustrato de PVC y empapada en agua. Cuando está mojada, puede manipularse durante horas antes de que se endurezca. Un molde de madera la sostiene mientras se seca durante 24 horas. Antes de que se haya secado, se cosen los bordes con hilos de colores vivos. Este material combina la cálida tersura de la tela y la estabilidad del hormigón frío, mientras que la superficie acabada conserva una apariencia blanda.

POR
Concreto costurado é um projeto inspirado pelos contrastes do material lona de concreto. Estes tamboretes são feitos dobrando-se lonas de concreto, um tecido previamente impregnado com uma camada de cimento e com um substrato de PVC, e depois foi embebido em água. Quando está molhado, pode ser manuseado durante algumas horas antes de endurecer. Um molde de madeira o fixa enquanto se seca durante 24 horas. Antes de se secar, costuram-se as bordas juntas com fio de cores brilhantes. O material combina suavidade quente do tecido e a estabilidade do concreto frio, enquanto a superfície acabada mantém sua aparência suave.

The stool is created from a half-wood, half-rubber mold. The wooden half gives the straight outer form and the wood-grain print from the rubber sheet gives a flowing impression on the interior. The pouring of the concrete is only strictly controlled on the exterior; the flexibility can be altered by the maker. The size of the object depends on the size of the mold used. The poured material is allowed to form itself on the non-rigid part. The flexibility of the mold and the process would allow the flowing texture to be used on the exterior of the stool as well.

FRA
Ce tabouret est fabriqué à l'aide d'un moule mi-bois mi-caoutchouc. La face externe des pieds issue de la partie bois est droite et lisse. La face interne, au contraire, est inégale et possède la texture que lui a conférée la partie en caoutchouc du moule. Le coulage du béton est strictement contrôlé et son mélange peut être plus ou moins malléable, selon l'effet recherché. La taille de l'objet est directement fonction de celle du moule. Le béton est coulé dans la partie souple du moule où il se solidifie. De par la flexibilité du moule et du procédé, on peut également le laisser couler à l'extérieur.

SSP
El taburete se crea con un molde de madera y caucho a partes iguales. La sección de madera aporta la forma externa recta, mientras que la textura granulada de la plancha de caucho transmite una impresión fluida del interior. El vertido de hormigón solo se controla estrictamente por fuera; el fabricante puede alterar la flexibilidad. El tamaño del objeto depende del tamaño del molde. El material vertido se solidifica en la parte que no es rígida. Gracias a la flexibilidad del molde y el proceso la textura flotante también puede aplicarse al exterior del taburete.

POURED WOOD

DESIGN FIRM
Henry Lawrence Studio

DESIGNER
Henry Lawrence Studio

PHOTOGRAPHY
Henry Lawrence Studio

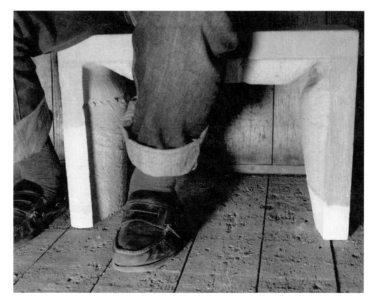

POR
O tamborete foi criado a partir de um molde metade de madeira e metade de borracha. Metade de madeira dá a forma exterior reta e a impressão de grão de madeira da lâmina e a borracha dá uma impressão fluida no interior. O derrame de concreto só está estritamente controlado no exterior; a flexibilidade pode ser alterada pelo fabricante. O tamanho do objeto depende do tamanho do molde usado. Permite-se que o material derramado tome forma na parte não rígida. A flexibilidade do molde e do processo permitiria que a textura flutuante se usasse também no exterior do tamborete.

THE COILING COLLECTION

DESIGN FIRM
Raw-Edges

DESIGNERS
Yael Mer & Shay Alkalay

PHOTOGRAPHY
Shay Alkalay

CLIENT
FAT Galerie Paris

The Coiling Collection is a series of interior objects made out of 100 percent woolen felt and silicon. A long strip of felt is coiled and shaped into a three-dimensional body. The natural softness of one side of the felt is kept, while the other side is saturated with silicon. The felt absorbs the silicon into its fibers and together they set into a hybrid material with a structural build. The idea was inspired by composite materials, a combination of bonding and structural materials, similar to reinforced concrete or the ancient cob, a material made from mud and straw that sets. The exhibition of the Coiling Collection at the FAT Galerie in Paris included seven new prototypes made out of 326 meters of felt in total.

TAILORED STOOL

DESIGN FIRM
Raw-Edges

DESIGNERS
Yael Mer & Shay Alkalay

PHOTOGRAPHY
Shay Alkalay

CLIENT
Cappellini

To make the Tailored Stool a technique similar to that used in the clothing industry is applied to furniture. A pattern is generated, and when assembled the resulting void is filled with foam. Just as a suit is altered to fit the client, this furniture is custom made and adapted to fit the user, whether they are tall, short, skinny, or fat. The process is unconventional for industrially produced furniture in that it proposes a construction technique without a mold. The pattern itself becomes both the defining surface and the mold. In a sense it is a reversal of upholstery, in which normally a skin is applied over the stuffing.

FRA
Pour fabriquer un tabouret Tailored Stool, on utilise une technique proche de la couture : on crée un patron. Lorsque la structure est montée, on remplit le vide avec de la mousse. Et, comme dans le cas d'un vêtement que l'on retouche pour qu'il siée parfaitement au client, le tabouret est adapté à l'utilisateur. Il est fabriqué sur mesure en fonction des particularités de la personne, qu'elle soit grande ou petite, maigre ou grosse. Le procédé de fabrication est plutôt inhabituel dans l'industrie du meuble, dans le sens où aucun moule n'est utilisé. C'est le patron qui devient à la fois la surface de référence et le moule. Le procédé est en quelque sorte à l'opposé de la tapisserie qui consiste à appliquer un revêtement sur un rembourrage.

ESP
En la confección del taburete a medida se aplica al mobiliario una técnica semejante a la que se emplea en la industria textil. Se diseña un patrón y cuando se monta se rellena el vacío resultante con espuma. Así como se hacen alteraciones en un traje para que le siente bien al cliente, este mueble se hace a medida para que se amolde a la estatura y la complexión del usuario. Este proceso es poco ortodoxo en la industria del mueble, en el sentido de que propone una técnica de fabricación en la que no se emplean moldes. El patrón se convierte al mismo tiempo en el molde y la superficie definidora. En cierto modo, es una trasposición de la tapicería, en la que suele aplicarse la piel sobre el relleno.

POR
Para fazer o Tamborete de alfaiate, aplica-se ao mobiliário uma técnica semelhante à usada na indústria da roupa. Gera-se um modelo e quando se monta o vazio resultante é preenchido com espuma. Tal como se reforma um terno para que se ajuste ao cliente, este móvel se personaliza e se adapta para ajustar-se ao usuário, tanto se forem altos, baixos, magros ou gordos. O processo não é convencional para o mobiliário produzido a nível industrial pelo fato de propor uma técnica de construção sem molde. O próprio modelo se converte tanto na superfície definidora como no molde. Em certo sentido, é uma virada do estofamento, em que normalmente se aplica uma pele sobre o recheio.

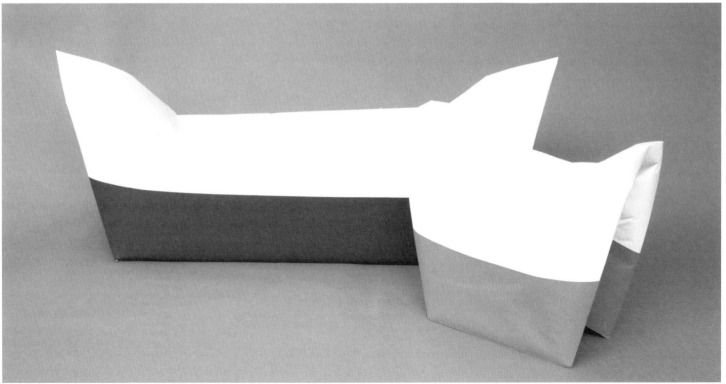

GAUDI CHAIR

DESIGN FIRM
Studio Geenen

DESIGNER
Bram Geenen

PHOTOGRAPHY
Bram Geenen

The Gaudi Chair is the follow-up to the Gaudi Stool, which was created in 2009. It was designed using the same method deployed by Antoni Gaudí, who made models using hanging chains that gave him an upside-down version of the strongest shape for his buildings. To be able to determine the structure of the chair's backrest a software script was also used. The script was based on three factors: firstly the distribution of forces across the surface of the chair; secondly the direction of forces that will define the direction of the ribs; and lastly the amount of force required to specify the height of a rib. The materials and techniques were chosen in order to create a lightweight chair. The surface is made of carbon fiber and the ribs are made of glass-filled nylon using selective laser sintering.

ESP
La silla Gaudi es la continuación del taburete Gaudí de 2009. El diseño emplea el mismo método que aplicaba Antoni Gaudí, que fabricaba modelos mediante cadenas colgantes con las que obtenía una versión invertida de la forma más robusta para sus edificios. Para determinar la estructura del respaldo de la silla también se ha utilizado un script de software basado en tres factores: la distribución de las fuerzas en la superficie de la silla, la dirección de las fuerzas que definen la dirección de los nervios y la fuerza necesaria para especificar la altura de estos. Se escogieron materiales y técnicas adecuados para una silla ligera. La superficie es de fibra de carbono y los nervios de nailon de fibra de vidrio con sinterizado de láser selectivo.

FRA
La chaise Gaudi Chair s'inscrit dans la droite ligne du tabouret Gaudi Stool créé en 2009. Elle a été conçue à l'aide de la méthode de chaînettes qu'employait Antoni Gaudí pour suspendre à l'envers ses maquettes afin d'étudier la solidité des bâtiments. Pour mettre au point la structure du dossier de la chaise, l'artiste a également fait appel à un script informatique basé sur trois paramètres : la répartition des forces sur toute la surface de la chaise ; la direction de ces forces qui définirait celle des nervures ; et la quantité des forces exercées qui commanderait la hauteur des nervures. Ces matériaux et techniques ont été choisis dans le but de créer une chaise légère. Sa surface est en fibre de carbone et les nervures sont en nylon rempli de verre et produites par frittage sélectif laser. Le but du projet était de voir comment les nouvelles technologies pouvaient reposer sur des concepts simples et logiques. Celui choisi ici a fait ses preuves depuis plus d'un siècle tant pour la beauté que pour la solidité des structures qu'il a inspirées.

POR
A cadeira Gaudí é a continuação do tamborete Gaudi, criado em 2009. Foi desenhado usando-se o mesmo método usado por Antoni Gaudí, que fez modelos utilizando correntes suspensas que lhe deram uma versão boca para baixo da forma mais forte para seus edifícios. Para poder determinar a estrutura do apoio da cadeira, usou-se também um software. Baseia em três fatores: primeiro, a distribuição de forças através da superfície da cadeira; segundo, a direção das forças que definirão a direção das nervuras; e, por último, a quantidade de força necessária para especificar a altura de uma nervura. Os materiais e técnicas foram escolhidos para criar uma cadeira ligeira. A superfície é feita de fibra de carbono e as nervuras são feitos de nylon com fibra de vidro usando o sinterizado de laser seletivo.

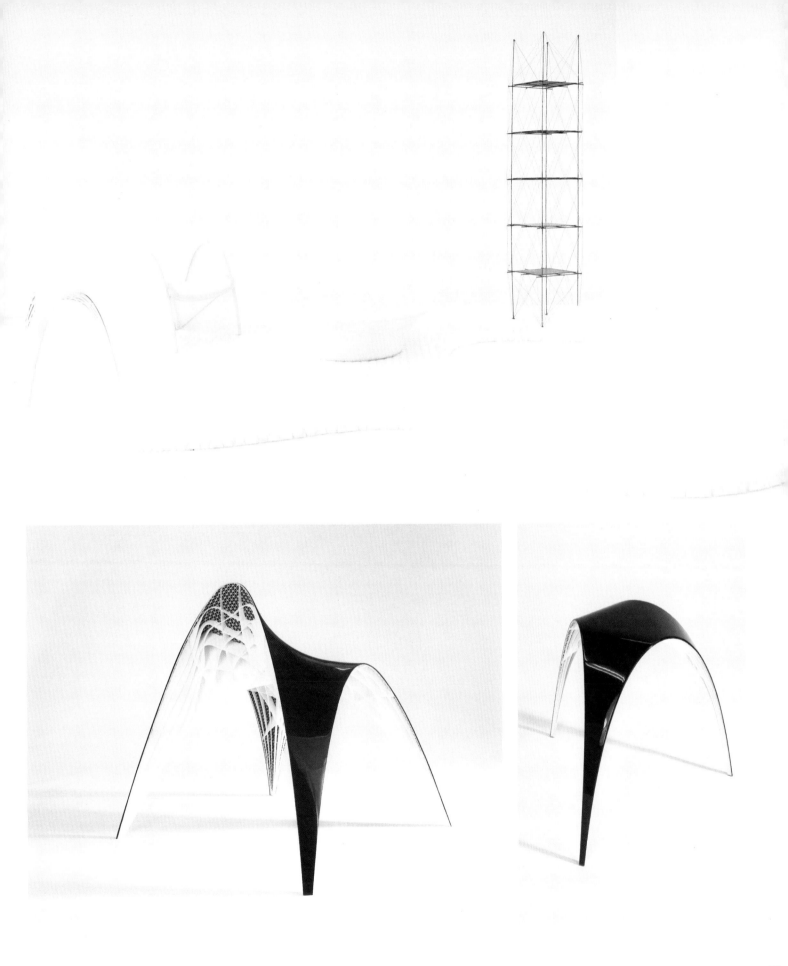

C BENCH

DESIGN FIRM
Outdoorz Gallery

DESIGNER
Peter Donders

PHOTOGRAPHER
Studio Leyssen

This contemporary, organic piece is made by twisting a single carbon-fiber string around a form that is then removed. The resulting structure is airy yet incredibly strong and has been aptly described as "calligraphy in 3D." Currently the ultimate material available in terms of its weight-to-strength ratio, carbon fiber is used to produce Formula One race cars and the highest-quality sporting equipment, as well as the chassis of space crafts. There are just ten pieces in this exceptional, limited-edition series, which is suitable for both public and private spaces.

FRA
Ce siège contemporain est fabriqué à partir d'une seule fibre de carbone enroulée autour d'une forme qui est retirée après l'opération. La structure obtenue est à la fois aérienne et particulièrement solide. Elle a été comparée, avec raison, à de la calligraphie en 3D. À l'heure actuelle, le meilleur matériau en termes de rapport poids-résistance est la fibre de carbone, que l'on utilise pour fabriquer des Formule 1, du matériel de sport de très haute qualité et le châssis de navettes spatiales. Il n'existe que 10 exemplaires de ce banc exceptionnel dans cette série limitée, qui conviennent aussi bien pour un usage extérieur qu'intérieur.

ESP
Esta pieza orgánica y contemporánea se fabrica enrollando una tira de fibra de carbono alrededor de una forma que se elimina a continuación. La estructura resultante es liviana, pero extraordinariamente fuerte, y se ha descrito acertadamente como "caligrafía en 3D". La fibra de carbono, que actualmente es el material más vanguardista en términos de la ratio entre el peso y la fuerza, se utiliza en la fabricación de coches de Fórmula 1 y los mejores equipos deportivos, así como los chasis de las naves espaciales. Solo existen diez piezas en esta extraordinaria serie limitada, idónea tanto para espacios públicos como privados.

POR
Esta peça contemporânea e orgânica é feita retorcendo uma só tira de fibra de carbono em volta de uma forma que depois é eliminada. A estrutura resultante é leve, mas incrivelmente forte e foi descrita muito adequadamente como "caligrafia em 3D". Atualmente, o material mais vanguardista disponível em termos de sua ratio peso-força, as fibras de carbono são usadas para produzir carros de corrida Fórmula 1 e o equipamento esportivo da mais alta qualidade, assim como os chassis de naves espaciais. Só existem dez peças nesta série excepcional e de edição limitada, que é adequada tanto para espaços públicos como particulares.

PLUM
STOOL

DESIGN FIRM
Alvaro Uribe Design

DESIGNER
Alvaro Uribe

PHOTOGRAPHY
Alvaro Uribe

This stool is an investigation into carbon fiber and its possible usage in residential furniture. The objective of the product is to achieve lightness and performance. By bending the material in key stress points and creating structural ribs, the stool is created using the minimum amount of material, and weighs just three hundred grams. The form is inspired by leaf veins, which optimize the body of the leaf so it keeps its shape and resists wind and pressure. Likewise the bends of the stool create a structure which is natural and whose different parts blend together without the need for adhesives or welding. With a dynamic movement, similar to that of a ballet dancer, the stool reflects the possibilities within materials, natural forms, and industry.

ESP
Este taburete ahonda en las posibilidades de la fibra de carbono para la fabricación de muebles domésticos. El producto es liviano y funcional. Gracias a los recodos en los puntos clave de presión, así como a los nervios estructurales, el taburete solo utiliza el material imprescindible y apenas pesa trescientos gramos. La forma se inspira en las venas de las hojas, que optimizan el cuerpo de estas para que conserven la forma y resistan el viento y la presión. Del mismo modo, los recodos del taburete crean una estructura natural, cuyos componentes se funden sin adhesivos ni soldaduras. Con un movimiento dinámico, semejante al de una bailarina de ballet, el taburete refleja las posibilidades que encierran los materiales, las formas naturales y la industria.

FRA
Ce tabouret est le fruit de recherches sur la fibre de carbone et ses utilisations possibles dans le mobilier d'habitation. L'objectif ici était de concilier légèreté et solidité. Le matériau est plié au niveau de points de tension clés de manière à créer des nervures structurelles qui permettent de n'utiliser qu'une infime quantité de matériau, le tabouret ne pesant que 300 grammes. Sa forme s'inspire des nervures de feuilles qui constituent leur armature et les empêchent de se déformer en résistant au vent et à la pression. Les nervures du tabouret créent une structure naturelle dont les différentes parties se fondent harmonieusement sans qu'il y ait besoin de colle ou de soudure. La forme dynamique du tabouret, qui évoque une danseuse de ballet, est un exemple de ce que l'on peut faire en mariant matériaux, formes naturelles et technologie industrielle.

POR
Este tamborete é uma pesquisa em fibras de carbono e pode ser usado em mobiliário residencial. O objetivo do produto é conseguir leveza e execução. Ao dobrar o material pelos pontos-chave de pressão e criar nervuras estruturais, o tamborete foi criado usando a mínima quantidade de material e só pesa trezentos gramas. A forma é inspirada em veias de folhas, que otimizam o corpo da folha para que mantenha sua forma e resista ao vento e à pressão. Do mesmo modo, as curvas do tamborete criam uma estrutura natural, cujas partes diferentes se misturam sem necessidade de adesivos ou soldas. Com um movimento dinâmico, semelhante ao de uma dançarina de balé, o tamborete reflete as possibilidades dentro dos materiais, as formas naturais e o engenho.

DROMBO

DESIGN FIRM
La Mamba Studio

PHOTOGRAPHY
La Mamba Studio

CLIENT
Dune

Drombo was created by the designers from La Mamba Studio. Their motivation was to create furniture from coating materials; the end result in this case was pieces of furniture created out of a ceramic mesh. Freed from straight lines, a piece with a purely organic form arises.

FRA
Drombo a été créé par les designers de La Mamba Studio. Leur objectif était de concevoir du mobilier à partir de produits de revêtement. C'est ainsi qu'ils ont créé la collection Drombo à partir de mosaïques en céramique. Libérés des contraintes de la ligne droite, ils ont utilisé des courbes naturelles.

ESP
Los diseñadores de La Mamba Studio han creado Drombo con la intención de fabricar muebles con materiales que se emplean en revestimientos; el resultado final en este caso han sido muebles hechos con una malla de cerámica en los que se obtiene una forma puramente orgánica desprovista de líneas rectas.

POR
Drombo foi criado pelos designers da Mamba Studio. Sua motivação foi a de criar móveis a partir de materiais de cobertura; o resultado final neste caso foram os móveis criados a partir de uma mistura de cerâmica. Livre de linhas retas, esta peça emerge com uma forma puramente orgânica.

TRON ARMCHAIR

DESIGN FIRM
DROR

DESIGNER
Dror Benshetrit

PHOTOGRAPHY
Studio Dror

CLIENT
Cappellini

DESCRIPTION
Cappellini & Walt Disney Signature.

Conceived from the futuristic world of the Disney film *TRON: Legacy*, the TRON Armchair is a product that has been profoundly inspired by a material with features that are reminiscent of the rugged and rocky landscape of *TRON's* digital world. Produced using the rotomolding technique, made of 100 percent recyclable material, and suitable for both indoor and outdoor use, the armchair is available in different colors. Giulio Cappellini plays on the contrasts suggested by the film, and in particular the contrast between the real world and the world of *TRON:Legacy*. Natural elements embody this contraposition, so the dark grey of the "stone", and the white of the "air" represent the landscape of *TRON* and the safe house, while the light blue of "water" and the green of the "grass" represent the real world.

FRA

Semblant sortir tout droit du monde futuriste du film *TRON : l'héritage* de Disney, le fauteuil TRON est fabriqué dans une matière qui rappelle fortement le paysage tourmenté et rocailleux du monde numérique de TRON dont le meuble s'inspire. Produit par rotomoulage, le fauteuil est fabriqué dans un matériau 100 % recyclable, peut être utilisé en intérieur et en extérieur, et existe en différents coloris. Giulio Cappellini joue avec les contrastes suggérés dans le film, notamment sur celui existant entre le monde réel et celui de *TRON : l'héritage*. Les éléments de la nature incarnent cette dualité : le gris foncé de la pierre et le blanc de l'air représentent le paysage de TRON et le refuge, le bleu ciel de l'eau et le vert de l'herbe symbolisant le monde réel.

ESP

Basada en el mundo futurista de la película de Disney *TRON: Legacy*, el sillón TRON se inspira profundamente en un material cuyas características recuerdan al paisaje abrupto y rocoso del mundo digital de TRON. Producido mediante la técnica de rotomoldeado, con material 100 % reciclable, idóneo tanto para interiores como exteriores, el sillón está disponible en diferentes colores. Giulio Cappellini juega con los contrastes que sugiere la película, sobre todo entre el mundo real y el de *TRON: Legacy*. Los elementos naturales encarnan esta contraposición; así, el gris oscuro de la "piedra" y el blanco del "aire" representan el paisaje de TRON y el refugio, mientras que el azul claro del "agua" y el verde de la "hierba" representan el mundo real.

POR

Concebida a partir do mundo futurista do filme de Disney *TRON: Legacy*, a poltrona TRON é um produto que se inspirou profundamente num material com características que lembram a paisagem acidentada e rochosa do mundo digital de TRON. Produzida usando a técnica de moldagem rotativa, feita com material 100 % reciclável e adequada tanto ao uso interior como ao exterior, a poltrona está disponível em diferentes cores. Giulio Cappellini joga com os contrastes sugeridos pelo filme e, em particular, os contrastes entre o mundo real e o mundo de *TRON: Legacy*. Os elementos naturais encarnam esta contraposição; deste modo, o cinza escuro da "pedra" e o branco do "ar" representam a paisagem de TRON e a casa segura, enquanto o azul claro da "água" e o verde da "grama" representam o mundo real.

MUNKEN CUBE

DESIGN FIRM
JUNO

DESIGNERS
Björn Lux, Wolfgang Greter (JUNO),
Philipp Mainzer (e15)

PHOTOGRAPHY
Björn Lux

CLIENT
Arctic Paper / e15

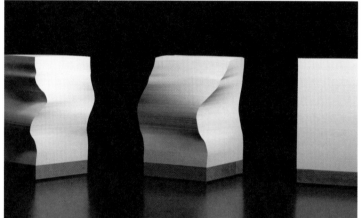

Arctic Paper, producer of graphic fine paper, and the furniture brand e15 are both looking to build on their current popularity. To help achieve this aim JUNO invented the Munken Cube, a design object that has set tongues wagging. From a six-centimeter-thick, solid oak base made by e15 2,200 sheets of high-quality 120-gram Munken paper rise up to form a forty-three-centimeter-high pad. For the Swedish paper manufacturer Arctic Paper the environment has a high significance. For the Munken Cube FSC-certified Munken Pure Rough 120-gram paper is used.

ESP
Arctic Paper, fabricantes de papel para las artes gráficas, y la marca de muebles e15 están tratando de aumentar su popularidad actual. Para ayudarles a conseguirlo, JUNO ha inventado el cubo Munken, un objeto de diseño que ha dado mucho que hablar. Consiste en una base de roble de seis centímetros de grosor, obra de e15, en la que se depositan 2.200 hojas de papel Munken de 120 gramos, obteniéndose un cuaderno de cuarenta y tres centímetros de altura. El cubo Munken utiliza papel rugoso de 120 gramos con certificado del FSC.

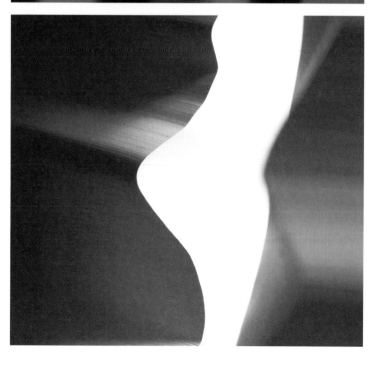

FRA
Arctic Paper, producteur de papier à dessin de qualité, et la marque de meuble e15 souhaitent tirer parti de leur notoriété. À cet effet, JUNO a inventé le Munken Cube, un objet design qui a fait couler beaucoup d'encre. Reposant sur un socle en chêne massif d'une épaisseur de 6 cm fabriqué par e15, une liasse de 2 200 feuilles de papier Munken 120 g de haute qualité forme un bloc de 43 cm de haut. L'environnement compte beaucoup pour le fabricant de papier suédois Arctic Paper. Pour fabriquer le Munken Cube, du papier Munken Pure Rough 120 g certifié FSC est utilisé.

POR
Artic Paper, produtor de papel fino gráfico, e a marca de móveis e15 procuram aumentar sua popularidade atual. Para os ajudar a atingir este objetivo, JUNO inventou o Cubo Munkem, um objeto de design que deu muito o que falar. A partir de uma base de carvalho sólido de seis centímetros de espessura feita pela e15, se levantam 2.200 folhas de papel de alta qualidade Munkem de 120 gramas, para formar um bloco de notas de quarenta e três centímetros de altura. Para o fabricante sueco de papel Artic Paper o ambiente é muito significativo. Para o Cubo Munkem, se usa papel de 120 gramas rugoso puro, com certificado FSC.

TOPO TABLES

DESIGN FIRM
NONdesigns, LLC

DESIGNERS
Scott Franklin & Miao Miao

PHOTOGRAPHY
Coy Koehler

CLIENT
NONdesigns, LLC.

TOPO is a series of Corian tables with built-in, reconfigurable landscapes. Plastic inserts drop into the table to create functional topographies. TOPO uses rapid prototyping technology in a way that enables each table to be different. It's a very simple design but the process of ordering one is a lot of fun. Our customers get to color in the areas that they want the inserts to be placed and then the CNC cuts out the holes. The inserts sit in the holes and can be swapped out and rearranged. When not in use, these functional landforms invert to become sculptural mountains. TOPO comes in three sizes: eight feet, six feet, and four-feet coffee table.

FRA

TOPO est une série de tables en Corian qui intègrent des paysages reconfigurables. Le plateau comporte des ouvertures prévues pour accueillir des petits bacs générant des topographies fonctionnelles. TOPO fait appel à la technologie de prototypage rapide qui permet de produire à chaque fois une table différente. Le concept est très simple et il est amusant de commander son propre modèle. Les clients colorent les zones où ils souhaitent placer les bacs et la machine numérique découpe les ouvertures correspondantes. On peut intervertir les bacs ou les placer à l'envers si l'on ne souhaite pas les remplir, pour créer des « collines ». TOPO est disponible en TOPO est disponible en trois tailles : 240 cm, 180 cm et 120 cm.

ESP

TOPO es una serie de mesas en las que se insertan paisajes incrustados que adoptan diversas configuraciones. Las inserciones de plástico crean topografías funcionales. TOPO emplea una tecnología de prototipado rápido para que cada mesa sea diferente. Se trata de un diseño sumamente sencillo, pero el proceso de compra es muy divertido. Nuestros clientes colorean los puntos en los que quieren que se hagan las inserciones y nosotros hacemos los orificios con una fresadora CNC. Las inserciones se depositan en estos orificios y es posible sacarlas y colocarlas de otra forma. Cuando no se usan, estos accidentes geográficos funcionales se invierten, convirtiéndose en montañas escultóricas. La serie TOPO está disponible en tres tamaños: mesita de café de 2,4 metros, 1,8 metros y 1,2 metros.

POR

TOUPEIRA é uma série de mesas com paisagens incrustadas e reconfiguráveis. Na mesa se recortam inserções de plástico para criar topografias funcionais. TOUPEIRA usa tecnologia prototípica rápida, de tal forma que permite que cada mesa seja diferente. É uma concepção muito simples, mas o processo de encomenda é muito divertido. Nossos clientes pintam as zonas onde querem que se coloquem as inserções e depois a CNC corta os furos. A inserção se mete nos furos e se pode retirar e recolocar. Quando não se usa, estes acidentes geográficos funcionais se invertem para se converter em montanhas esculturais. TOUPEIRA vem em três tamanhos: mesa de café de oito, seis e quatro pés.

SOFTSEATING
FANNING
STOOL

DESIGN FIRM
molo

DESIGNERS
Stephanie Forsythe & Todd MacAllen

PHOTOGRAPHY
molo

The inspiration for Softseating comes from a desire for flexible and spontaneous space-making. Softseating's magnetic ends allow it to connect to itself, forming a cylindrical stool or low table. Elements of the same size can also connect to one another to form long, winding benches, providing endless seating topographies. Made from a single material, the beauty of these pieces sits between the representative and the abstract, with the two creatively interchanging with one another. Designed for long-term use, over time the surface texture of Softseating's paper edges softens into a pleasing natural patina.

FRA
L'idée de Softseating est de proposer un siège capable de s'adapter à toutes les situations. Les côtés des modules sont magnétiques de manière à pouvoir les accoler les uns aux autres pour former, par exemple, un siège rond ou une table basse. On peut également relier des éléments de même taille pour constituer des bancs ondulant de la longueur voulue, et suivant une topographie modulable à l'infini. Softseating, fabriqué dans un seul matériau, est à mi-chemin entre le figuratif et l'abstrait, les deux esthétiques cohabitant en harmonie. Conçue pour durer, la texture de la surface des bords en papier de Softseating devient plus douce et se patine agréablement au fil des temps.

ESP
El taburete blando se inspira en el deseo de crear espacios flexibles y espontáneos. Gracias a sus extremos magnéticos puede conectarse formando un taburete cilíndrico o una mesita baja. Los elementos del mismo tamaño también pueden conectarse, componiendo bancos alargados y sinuosos que proporcionan un sinfín de topografías. Fabricadas con un solo material, la belleza de estas piezas se encuentra en los diálogos creativos entre lo representativo y lo abstracto. Diseñada para un uso duradero, con el tiempo se suaviza la textura de los bordes de papel, que adquieren una bonita pátina natural.

POR
A inspiração para Suave assento surge de um desejo de criar espaços flexíveis e espontâneos. Os cabos magnéticos de Suave assento permitem se conectar de novo, formando um tamborete cilíndrico ou uma mesa baixa. Os elementos do mesmo tamanho também podem se conectar um ao outro para formar bancos longos e serpenteantes, proporcionando infindáveis topografias de assento. Feito de um só material, a beleza destas peças encontra-se entre o figurativo e o abstrato, com os dois permutando-se criativamente. Desenhado para um uso em longo prazo, com o tempo a textura de superfície das bordas de papel de Suave assento se suaviza numa agradável pátina natural.

FLOOD STOOL

DESIGN FIRM
Azúa Moline

DESIGNERS
Martín Azúa & G. Moline

PHOTOGRAPHY
Martín Azúa

CLIENT
Mobles 114

This stool for outdoor and indoor use is made from 100 percent recyclable polyethylene using rotomolding. Inspired by nature, the sculptural forms are achieved in a compromise between the technology and the material. The attained aesthetic is naturally simple.

ESP
Este taburete de interior y exterior está hecho de polietileno 100 % reciclable mediante un proceso de rotomoldeado. Inspirado en la naturaleza, las formas escultóricas nacen del compromiso entre la tecnología y el material, consiguiéndose una estética naturalmente sencilla.

FRA
Ce siège pour extérieur et intérieur est fabriqué en polyéthylène 100 % recyclable suivant la technique du rotomoulage. Inspirées par la nature, ses formes sculpturales résultent d'un bon compromis entre la technologie et le matériau. L'esthétique de l'ensemble est naturellement dépouillée.

POR
Este tamborete para uso exterior e interior é feito de polietileno 100 % reciclável usando a moldagem rotativa. Inspirado na natureza, conseguem-se as formas esculturais num compromisso entre a tecnologia e o material. A estética conseguida é naturalmente simples.

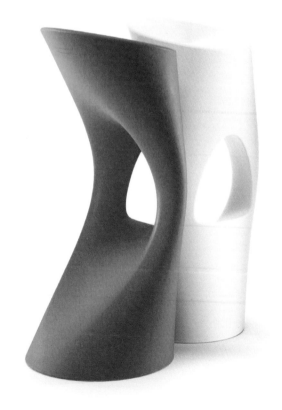

THE INNER LIFE

DESIGN FIRM
Martín Azúa Studio

DESIGNER
Martín Azúa

PHOTOGRAPHY
Martín Azúa

The Inner Life is a series of useful objects that can harbor life of both a vegetal and an animalistic nature. Martín Azúa continues to work on the research he started with the project Natural Finish in 1999, when he placed jars made of porous ceramics in river beds, allowing them to collect a natural stain. With The Inner Life he presents an integration of natural processes in everyday life: life inside objects.

FRA
The Inner Life est une série d'objets utiles pouvant servir de refuge aussi bien à des végétaux que des animaux. Martín Azúa continue à travailler sur le projet de recherche Natural Finish démarré en 1999, où il avait déposé des jarres en céramique poreuse dans le lit de rivières pour qu'elles acquièrent une patine naturelle. Sa série The Inner Life représente l'intégration de processus naturels dans notre quotidien : c'est la vie au cœur des objets.

ESP
La vida interior es una serie de objetos útiles que albergan vida vegetal y animal. Martín Azúa continúa trabajando en la investigación que comenzara en 1999 con el proyecto "Acabado natural", depositando jarrones de cerámica porosa en el lecho de los ríos para que adquiriesen manchas naturales. Con La vida interior presenta una integración de los procesos naturales en la vida cotidiana: la vida dentro de los objetos.

POR
A vida interior é uma série de objetos úteis que podem hospedar vida de natureza tanto vegetal como animal. Martín Azúa continua a trabalhar na pesquisa que começou com o projeto Acabamento natural em 1999, quando colocou copos de cerâmica porosa em leitos de rio, permitindo-lhes adquirir uma mancha natural. Com A vida interior, apresenta uma integração dos processos naturais na vida cotidiana: a vida dentro dos objetos.

PEACOCK CHAIR

DESIGN FIRM
DROR

DESIGNER
Dror Benshetrit

The Peacock Chair is created out of
three sheets of felt and a minimal metal
frame. The folds of the felt are woven
tightly to form a structured yet incredibly
comfortable lounge chair, with no sewing
or upholstery involved. The Peacock
recently entered the permanent collection
of the Metropolitan Museum in New York
and is now on display at the Design Gallery
of the museum.

PHOTOGRAPHY
Studio Dror

CLIENT
Cappellini

ESP
La silla pavo real se compone de tres
retales de fieltro y una reducida estructura
metálica. Los pliegues del fieltro están
estrechamente entretejidos formando una
butaca estructurada, pero increíblemente
cómoda, sin costuras ni tapicería que ha
ingresado recientemente en la colección
permanente del Museo Metropolitano de
Nueva York, donde se exhibe en la Galería
de Diseño.

FRA
Le fauteuil Peacock est constitué de
trois plaques en feutre montées sur un
cadre métallique très simple. Les plis du
feutre sont tissés très serrés de manière
à former un fauteuil à la fois structuré et
incroyablement moelleux. Il n'y a aucune
couture ni rembourrage. Le fauteuil
Peacock fait partie depuis peu de la
collection permanente du Metropolitan
Museum de New York et est exposé
actuellement à la Design Gallery du musèe.

POR
O Poltrona peru real foi criada a partir de
três lâminas de feltro e uma estrutura
metálica mínima. As dobras do feltro estão
entretecidas firmemente para formar um
poltrona estruturada, mas incrivelmente
cômoda, sem envolver costuras nem
estofamento. O Peru real acaba de entrar
na coleção permanente do Metropolitan
Museum de Nova York e agora está
exposto na Galeria de Design do museu.

PRESSED CHAIR

DESIGNER
Harry Thaler

PHOTOGRAPHY
Jäger & Jäger, Studio Harry Thaler

The uniform materiality of this seat has its source in the notion of 100 percent reusability. Aluminum is obtained from ore, the most commonly present metal in the earth's crust; it is notable for its corrosion resistance and unlimited reuse. In designing the Pressed Chair Harry Thaler aimed to instill it with the utmost tactile qualities, practical convenience, and environmental considerations. Furthermore, almost no waste is created in the production of Pressed Chair; the leftover aluminum is worked into a simple stool comprised of three components connected with metal screws.

ESP

La uniformidad de la silla se inspira en el concepto de la reutilización 100%. El aluminio se obtiene de la mena, el metal más común de la corteza terrestre, que destaca por su resistencia a la corrosión y la reutilización ilimitada. Al diseñar la silla prensada, Harry Thaler ha tenido como objetivo infundirle las mayores cualidades táctiles, así como el pragmatismo y las consideraciones medioambientales. Además, la fabricación apenas genera residuos; con el aluminio desechado se obtiene un taburete sencillo, con tres componentes que se conectan mediante tornillos metálicos.

FRA

L'homogénéité de ce siège repose sur la notion de matériau réutilisable à 100 %. L'aluminium, extrait d'un minerai, est le métal le plus abondant de l'écorce terrestre. Il est connu pour sa résistance à la corrosion et son réemploi illimité. Lorsqu'il a conçu le fauteuil Pressed Chair, Harry Thaler a voulu conjuguer confort, commodité et respect de l'environnement. En outre, la fabrication du fauteuil ne génère pratiquement aucun résidu. L'aluminium restant est travaillé de façon à produire un tabouret très simple formé de trois éléments assemblés à l'aide de vis.

POR

A materialidade uniforme deste assento origina-se na noção de 100 % reutilização. O alumínio é obtido do minério, o metal mais comum presente na crosta da Terra; destaca-se por sua resistência à corrosão e reutilização ilimitada. Ao projetar a Cadeira prensada, Harry Thaler teve como objetivo infundir nela as melhores qualidades táteis, comodidade prática e considerações ambientais. Além disso, quase não se criam resíduos na produção da Cadeira prensada; o alumínio restante é trabalhado para criar um tamborete simples que possui três componentes conectados com parafusos metálicos.

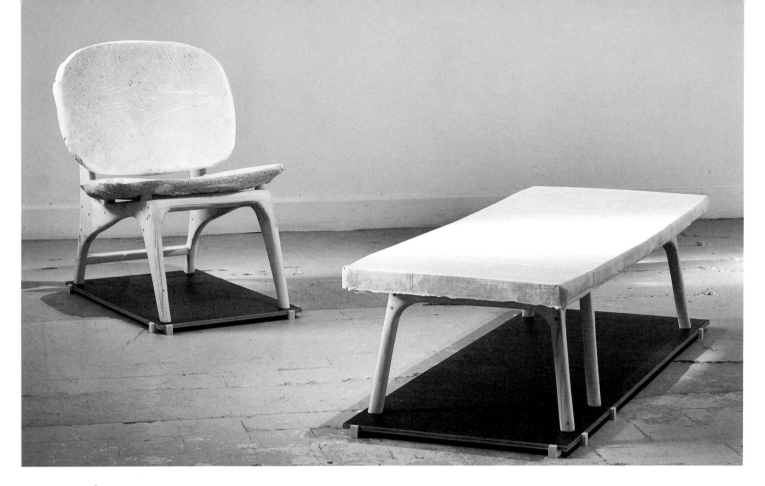

UNPØLISHED

DESIGN FIRM
Studio Dik Scheepers

DESIGNER
Dik Scheepers

PHOTOGRAPHY
Kristof Vrancken & Dik scheepers

CLIENT
Toegepast 16, Z33

Dik Scheepers became interested in the material paper crete because it seemed so simple to make yourself. In essence you only need to mix together paper and cement and you have your own homemade material. For the exhibition *Toegepast 16* at Z33, Belgium, Dik experimented with and formulated his own recipe, and by combining it with white wood he made this experimental furniture collection.

FRA

Dik Scheepers s'est intéressé au liant papier, ou papier-ciment, parce qu'il avait l'air facile à réaliser soi-même. En gros, il suffit de mélanger du papier et du ciment pour disposer d'un matériau fait maison. Pour l'exposition *Toegepast 16* au centre Z33, en Belgique, Dik a fait plusieurs essais et mis au point sa propre recette. Il a associé le papier-ciment à du bois blanc pour fabriquer cette collection de meubles expérimentale.

ESP

Dik Scheepers se interesó por el hormigón de papel porque le parecía sencillo fabricarlo. Básicamente, solo hay que mezclar papel y cemento para hacerlo en casa. El hormigón de papel sigue siendo un material experimental que se elabora principalmente con papel desechado. Es barato, versátil y ligero, pero cuesta procesarlo y tarda mucho en secarse. Tiene un tacto agradable y pueden obtenerse versiones diferentes empleando diversos tipos de papel. En la exposición *Toegepast 16* de Z33, en Bélgica, Dik experimentaba con una receta que había formulado él mismo y ha creado esta colección de muebles experimentales combinándola con madera blanca.

POR

Dez Scheepers interessou-se pelo material concreto de papel porque parecia tão fácil a ponto de qualquer um poder fazê-lo. Essencialmente, você só necessita misturar papel e cimento e já tem seu próprio material caseiro. Para a exposição *Toegepast 16* em Z33, Bélgica, Dik experimentou e formulou sua própria receita e, ao combinar o mesmo com madeira, branca, fez esta coleção experimental de mobiliário.

TRASH CUBE

DESIGN FIRM
Nicolas Le Moigne

DESIGNER
Nicolas Le Moigne

PHOTOGRAPHY
Tonatiuh Ambrosetti & Daniela Droz

CLIENT
Eternit (Schweiz) AG

The Swiss designer Nicolas Le Moigne has collaborated with fiber-cement company Eternit to create Trash Cube, a project that uses raw, recycled material to produce new stools. With a width and length of thirty-one centimeters and a height of thirty-six centimeters, the stools, which use leftover cement and fibers produced by Eternit, were designed to have the most basic form while using as many scraps as possible. Each piece goes through a metamorphic stage where the raw material is condensed and sculpted to the mold. While the overall shape remains relatively unchanged, the cubes are all unique, changing in appearance depending on how the discarded material settles.

ESP
El diseñador suizo Nicolas Le Moigne ha colaborado con los fabricantes de fibrocemento Eternit en la creación del cubo de basura, un proyecto en el que se emplean materiales toscos, reciclados, para producir nuevos taburetes. Con 31 centimetros de largo y ancho y 36 centimetros de alto, los taburetes de cemento sobrante y fibras de Eternit se han diseñado para que tengan una forma muy básica, utilizando todos los desechos posibles. Las piezas atraviesan una etapa metamórfica, donde la materia prima se condensa y se moldea. Aunque la forma se mantiene relativamente intacta, cada cubo es único y cambia de aspecto en función de cómo se asienta el material desechado.

FRA
Le designer suisse Nicolas Le Moigne a collaboré avec la compagnie de fibrociment Eternit pour le projet Trash Cube qui utilise des matériaux bruts et recyclés pour produire des tabourets neufs. D'une largeur et d'une longueur de 31 cm pour une hauteur de 36 cm, les tabourets fabriqués à partir du surplus de ciment et de fibres produits par Eternit, ont été conçus de manière à rassembler le plus de déchets possibles dans la forme la plus simple qui soit. Chaque unité passe par une étape de métamorphose où le matériau brut est condensé et sculpté dans le moule. Si la forme est pratiquement identique d'un tabouret à l'autre, les cubes sont tous des pièces uniques, car leur aspect dépend de la manière dont les déchets se sont agglomérés.

POR
O designer suiço Nicolas Lhe Moigne colaborou com a empresa Eternit de fibrocimento para criar o Cubo de resíduos, um projeto que usa material em bruto, reciclado, para produzir novos tamboretes. Com uma largura e comprimento de trinta e um centímetros e uma altura de trinta e seis centímetros, os tamboretes, que usam sobras de cimento e fibras produzidas pela Eternit, foram desenhados para ter a forma mais básica, ao mesmo tempo em que são usados tantos restos quanto seja possível. Cada peça passa por uma etapa metamórfica, onde a matéria-prima é condensada e esculpida ao molde. Enquanto a forma total permanece relativamente sem alterações, todos os cubos são únicos, alterando sua aparência conforme o lugar em que se põe o material rejeitado.

DUNE

DESIGN FIRM
Studio Rainer Mutsch

DESIGNER
Rainer Mutsch

Produced by the company Eternit, the used fiber cement used to make Dune is a very durable, fully recyclable, and sustainable material consisting of 100 percent natural materials such as cellulose fibers and water. It took over two years of development time in order to get the maximum stability out of the three-dimensional, deformed, fiber-cement panels. The geometry of the chair supports its stability through its controlled expansion and compression of the cellulose-based material, which results in an impressive load capacity of around one thousand kilograms on the seating surface. Since Dune has been designed as highly modular and indefinitely expandable system, it is capable of fitting into most spatial situations.

FRA
Produit par la société Eternit, la série Dune est en fibrociment durable, 100 % recyclable et composé uniquement de matériaux naturels comme la cellulose et l'eau. Il a fallu plus de deux ans pour optimiser la stabilité des panneaux de fibrociment mis en forme. Celle de la chaise dérive de l'expansion et de la compression contrôlées du matériau à base de cellulose qui lui confère une capacité de charge étonnante de près d'une tonne au niveau de l'assise. Le système Dune étant modulaire et extensible à l'infini, il peut s'adapter à pratiquement tous les espaces possibles.

ESP
El fibrocemento usado Eternit que se ha empleado en la fabricación de Duna es un material muy duradero, completamente reciclable y sostenible que se compone de materiales 100 % naturales, como fibras de celulosa y agua. Han sido necesarios más de dos años de desarrollo para que los paneles de fibrocemento deformados tridimensionales fueron lo más estables posible. La geometría de la silla se mantiene estable mediante la expansión y la compresión controladas de este material con base de celulosa, obteniéndose como resultado una extraordinaria capacidad de carga de aproximadamente una tonelada en la superficie del asiento. Duna está diseñada como un sistema modular que puede expandirse indefinidamente, de manera que se adapta a la mayoría de las situaciones espaciales.

POR
Produzido pela empresa Eternit, o cimento de fibra usada que se empregou para fazer Duna é um material muito duradouro, totalmente reciclável, e sustentável, que consiste em materiais 100 % naturais, como fibras de celulose e água. O desenvolvimento demorou mais de dois anos a fim de se conseguir a máxima estabilidade dos painéis tridimensionais, deformados e de cimento de fibra. A geometria da cadeira suporta sua estabilidade através de sua expansão e compressão controladas do material baseado em celulose, o qual dá como resultado uma impressionante capacidade de carga de cerca de mil quilos na superfície de assento. Como se concebeu Duna como um sistema altamente modular e indefinidamente expansível, é capaz de se ajustar à maioria de situações espaciais.

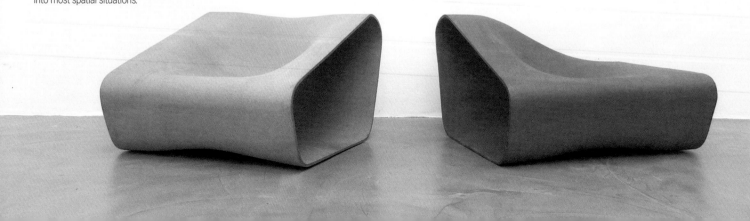

ALIEN

DESIGNER
Jonas Jurgaitis

PRODUCER
Sedes Regia

PHOTOGRAPHY
t&v | Creep Photographers & Cyclopes

Alien is made of molded polyurethane "dreads" on a plywood frame with an armrest of solid wood, lacquered and polished to high gloss. There is a certain tension between traditionally crafted hardwood and hi-tech upholstery fabrics, and a closer look reveals subtle details and a quality of craftsmanship. In some cases the tips of the unfriendly looking hanks are humanized with Swarovski jewelry or even LED lights.

FRA
Alien est composé de « racines » en polyuréthane moulé disposées sur une structure en contreplaqué dotée d'un accoudoir en bois massif laqué et poli pour un effet ultrabrillant. Le bois travaillé de manière artisanale et les tissus d'ameublement de haute technologie ne font pas forcément bon ménage, mais il suffit d'examiner Alien de plus près pour noter certains détails subtils et signes de qualité de fabrication. Sur certains modèles, les boudins sont agrémentés de bijoux Swarovski ou de diodes électroluminescentes à leurs extrémités.

ESP
Alien se compone de "trenzas" de poliuretano moldeado sobre una estructura de madera contrachapada y un reposabrazos de madera barnizada con un esmalte reluciente. Existe cierta tensión entre la madera dura tallada con métodos tradicionales y los tejidos de la tapiceria de tecnología punta y una mirada atenta revela detalles sutiles y una artesanía excelente. En algunos casos se han humanizado las puntas de los temibles mechones con joyas de Swarovski o incluso con luces LED.

POR
Alienígena é feito de "terrores" de poliuretano moldado sobre uma estrutura de compensado com um apoio de braços de madeira sólida, envernizada e polida com esmalte brilhante. Existe certa tensão entre a madeira dura, talhada tradicionalmente, e os tecidos de estofamento de tecnologia de ponta, e um olhar mais próximo revela detalhes sutis e uma qualidade artesanal. Em alguns casos, as pontas das frias mechas se humanizam com joalheria Swarovski ou inclusive luzes LED.

TUFTY

DESIGNER
Jonas Jurgaitis

PRODUCER
Sedes Regia

PHOTOGRAPHY
t&v | Creep Photographers

Tufty does not really require much care, either as a plant or as a seat. Just love and attention. And it is still growing—on us. Tufty seems to be composed—or constituted—of a hard, veneered shell and some hard-looking but soft-cored spikes that are easily bent for convenience. Work your way through them and get hugged.

FRA
Tufty ne requiert aucun soin particulier, il faut juste l'aimer. Cette plante continue toujours à pousser, à nous pousser à l'adopter. Tufty ressemble à un pot en contreplaqué d'où sortent des tiges qui ont l'air rigide mais sont souples et se plient à notre convenance. Asseyez-vous sans crainte et laissez-vous envelopper.

ESP
Lo cierto es que Tufty no requiere demasiados cuidados como planta ni como asiento. Tan solo amor y atención. Y continúa creciendo con nosotros. Tufty consiste, o más bien se compone de una cáscara dura revestida y unas espinas de apariencia agresiva pero en el fondo blandas, que se doblan fácilmente. Ábrase camino a través de ellas para que lo abracen.

POR
Na realidade, Tufty não precisa de muito cuidado, nem como planta nem como assento. Só amor e atenção. E ainda cresce —conosco. Tufty parece ser composta ou constituída de uma casca dura e chapeada e de umas pontas de aparência dura, mas coração suave, que se dobram facilmente conforme convenha. Abra caminho através delas e deixe-se abraçar.

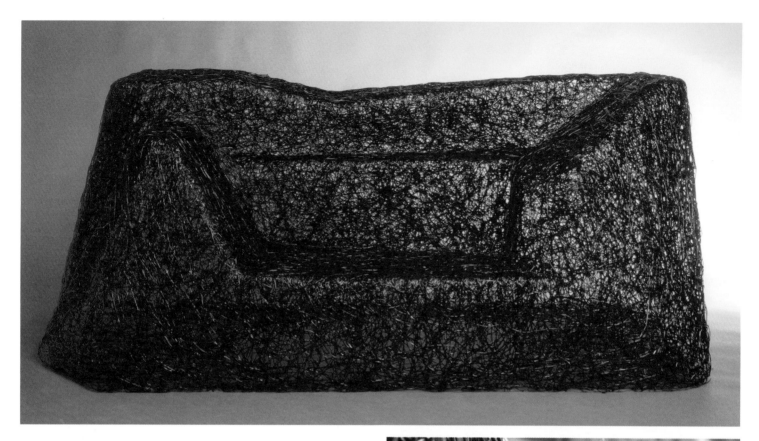

MAGIC MAGNUS MOUNTAIN

DESIGN FIRM
Studio / Magnus Sangild

DESIGNER
Magnus Sangild

PHOTOGRAPHY
Magnus Sangild

This furniture is inspired by nature's rocky formations and situations where people interact with them. This could be a situation where nature provides shelter or an opportunity to relax upon physical hardships. Often situations like these are accompanied by feelings of comfort and contemplation. In the midst of nature it is possible to enjoy yourself and relax. The rawness and comprehensiveness of rocks makes it hard to abstract from the surroundings you are in. But if you take a certain element out of nature and place it in a new context the experience of functionality within the design is enhanced. The shape has explicit references to the natural elements it is inspired by, but the visual identity of the furniture presents itself in a very powerful way.

FRA
Ce mobilier s'inspire des formations rocheuses que l'on trouve dans la nature et des situations où l'on recherche la proximité des rochers, par exemple, pour s'abriter ou se reposer après un effort. Dans ces moments-là, on se sent bien et d'une humeur plutôt contemplative. On passe un bon moment en pleine nature et l'on se détend. En raison de la rudesse du décor et de l'immensité des rochers, on a du mal à faire abstraction du paysage. Mais si l'on prend un élément quelconque de la nature et qu'on le place hors de son contexte, l'impression de fonctionnalité du design se renforce. La forme ici fait explicitement référence aux éléments de la nature qui l'inspirent, mais confère au meuble une identité visuelle d'une grande force.

ESP
Este mueble se inspira en las formaciones rocosas naturales y las situaciones en las que interactuamos con ellas, como por ejemplo una situación en la que la naturaleza nos ofrece un refugio o sencillamente la ocasión de relajarnos frente a las dificultades físicas. A menudo las situaciones como estas están acompañadas de sentimientos de confort y contemplación. Podemos relajarnos y disfrutar en medio de la naturaleza. Las rocas son tan toscas y tan amplias que nos cuesta abstraernos del entorno que nos rodea. Pero si sacamos un elemento de la naturaleza y lo depositamos en un nuevo contexto aumenta la experiencia de la función que subyace dentro del diseño. La forma tiene referencias explícitas a los elementos naturales en los que se ha inspirado, pero la identidad visual del mueble se presenta de una manera muy poderosa.

POR
Este móvel inspira-se nas formações rochosas da natureza e em situações em que as pessoas interagem com elas. Poder-se-ia tratar da situação onde a natureza proporciona abrigo ou uma oportunidade para se relaxar das dificuldades físicas. Frequentemente, situações como estas vão acompanhadas por sensações de comodidade e contemplação. No meio da natureza é possível desfrutar e se relaxar. A crueza e a amplidão das rochas dificulta a abstração do ambiente que nos rodeia. Mas, se tomamos certo elemento fora da natureza e o colocarmos num novo contexto, aumenta a experiência de funcionalidade dentro do design. A forma tem referências explícitas aos elementos naturais que a inspiram, mas a identidade visual do móvel se apresenta de forma muito poderosa.

SUCCESSION

DESIGN FIRM
Studio Fredrik Färg

DESIGNER
Fredrik Färg

PHOTOGRAPHY
Studio Fredrik Färg

Dressed in leather and textiles, the stools and cupboards in the Succession collection were brought to life through a series of processes. Their bases are made of an innovative composition of materials and have been upholstered with leather and textiles and had ropes tied around them before being baked. When the rope is cut away, the result is a seam-free, sophisticated, and refined pattern.

ESP
Los taburetes y armarios forrados de tela y piel de la colección Sucesión han cobrado vida mediante una serie de procesos. Las bases están hechas de una innovadora composición de materiales y tapizadas con tela y piel y las han envuelto con cuerdas antes de cocerlas. Cuando se cortan las cuerdas, el resultado que se obtiene es un modelo desprovisto de costuras, sofisticado y refinado.

FRA
Revêtus de cuir et de tissu, les tabourets et les meubles étagères de la collection Succession sont le produit de toute une série d'opérations. Leur structure est une composition novatrice de matériaux. Un fois recouverts de cuir et de tissu, ils sont entourés d'une corde avant de passer au four. Une fois la corde coupée, on obtient un motif sophistiqué, sans couture et raffiné.

POR
Vestidos de pele e tecidos, os tamboretes e armários da coleção Sucessão nasceram através de uma série de processos. Suas bases são feitas de uma composição inovadora de materiais e foram estofados com couro e tecidos e cordas foram amarradas em volta deles antes de os cozinhar. Quando se corta a corda, o resultado é um modelo livre de costuras, sofisticado e refinado.

AUTRES APPROCHES ÉCOLOGIQUES

Le design écologique est une approche de la conception de produits qui tient compte de l'impact environnemental. Outre les matériaux recyclés et réemployés et les nouvelles technologies appliquées à la création de meubles présentées dans cet ouvrage, il existe de multiples façons d'aborder le design.

04

POR

OUTROS ENFOQUES ECO

O design eco é um enfoque ao design de produtos que tenham uma consideração especial por seu impacto ambiental. Além dos assuntos de materiais reciclados e reutilizados, materiais naturais e novas tecnologias usadas no design de móveis que foram apresentados neste trabalho, existem muitos outros possíveis enfoques ao design.

ESP

OTRAS TENDENCIAS ECOLÓGICAS

La tendencia del diseño ecológico tiene en consideración especial el impacto de los productos en el medio ambiente. Además de las cuestiones de los materiales reciclados y reutilizados, los materiales naturales y las nuevas tecnologías que se han aplicado al diseño de los muebles que hemos presentado en esta obra, existen muchas otras tendencias en el diseño.

OTHER ECO APPROACHES

Eco design is an approach to designing products that has a special consideration for their environmental impact. In addition to the themes of recycled and reused materials, natural materials, and new technologies used in furniture design that have been presented in this work, there are many other possible approaches to design.

SPINNING CHAIR ACCELERATOR

DESIGN FIRM
BOREALIS

DESIGNER
Jaanus Orgusaar

PHOTOGRAPHY
BOREALIS

The inspiration for the Spinning Chair Accelerator came from the CERN accelerator. The vibration from the spinning of the metal ball inside awakens your spirit and renews your cells. After six spins you end up where you started. The curvy top of the chair is bent from a single, flat sheet of four-millimeter plywood, an extremely thin yet strong surface due to its clever construction.

FRA
Le fauteuil Spinning Chair Accelerator s'inspire de l'accélérateur de particules du CERN. La vibration transmise par la sphère en métal qu'il renferme éveille l'esprit et renouvelle les cellules. Après six tours, on revient au point de départ. L'arrondi est obtenu en pliant le panneau en contreplaqué de 4 mm d'épaisseur qui constitue le corps du fauteuil. Le matériau est mince mais très résistant grâce au mode d'élaboration intelligent.

ESP
La silla giratoria aceleradora se inspira en el acelerador CERN. La vibración que producen las rotaciones de la bola metálica que lleva dentro despierta el espíritu y renueva las células. Al cabo de seis vueltas, se acaba en el mismo punto donde se ha empezado. La curva superior de la silla se obtiene doblando una plancha lisa de madera contrachapada de cuatro milímetros, una superficie extremadamente delgada y sin embargo fuerte gracias a su astuta construcción.

POR
A inspiração para o Acelerador em cadeira giratória surgiu do acelerador CERN. A vibração proveniente dos giros da bola metálica em seu interior desperta o espírito e renova as células. Depois de seis rotações, a pessoa acaba onde começou. A curva superior da cadeira dobra-se a partir de uma única lâmina plana de compensado de quatro milímetros, uma superfície extremamente fina e simultaneamente forte devido à sua construção inteligente.

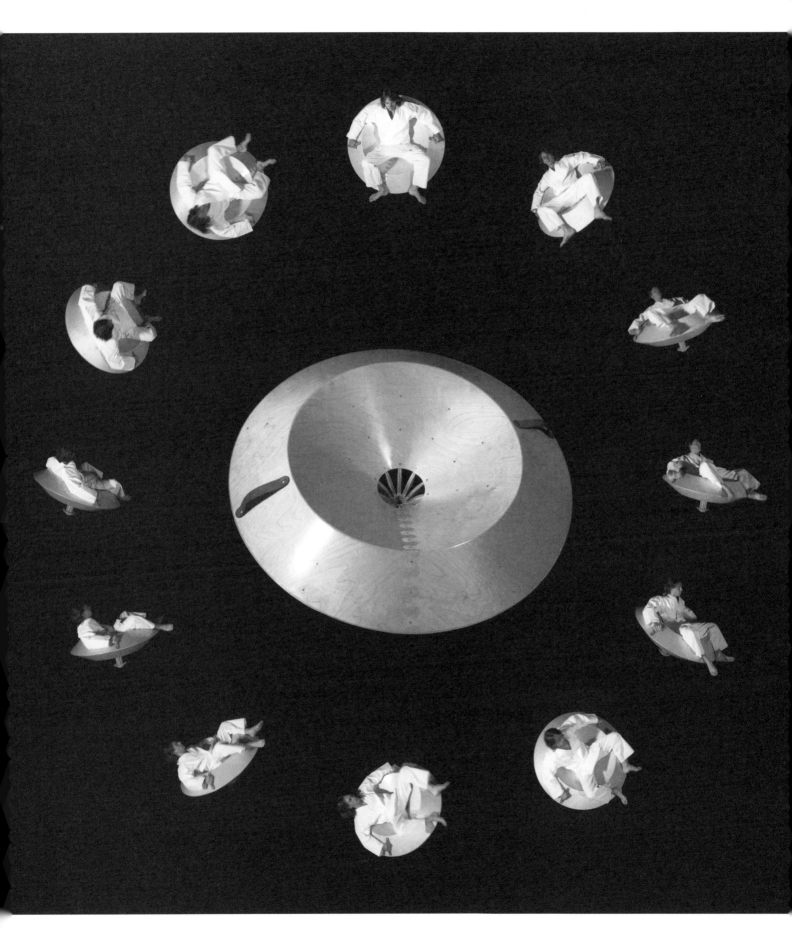

DARWIN CHAIR

DESIGN FIRM
Sagmeister Inc.

DESIGNERS
Stefan Sagmeister, Joris Laarman,
Paul Fung, Mark Pernice, Joe Shouldice,
Ben Bryant

PHOTOGRAPHY
Johannes vam Assem for Droog

The Darwin Chair utilizes a free-swinging
structure that includes about two
hundred sheets of attached prints. As
the top sheet gets dirty the user simply
rips it off, thereby transforming the
chair's appearance. As more and more
sheets are torn off the perforation forms
a comfortable headrest.

FRA
La chaise Darwin utilise une structure
à oscillation libre sur laquelle sont
fixées environ 200 feuilles à motifs
imprimés. Lorsque la feuille en cours
est sale, on l'arrache et on découvre
ainsi une nouvelle feuille conférant
un « look » totalement différent à la
chaise. À mesure que les feuilles sont
arrachées, les « souches » créent un
repose-tête de plus en plus confortable.

ESP
La silla Darwin emplea una estructura
de balanceo libre que incluye unas
doscientas impresiones adjuntas de
tal manera que cuando la primera se
ensucia, se arranca por las buenas,
transformando de esta forma la
apariencia de la silla. A medida que
se arrancan las capas sucesiva, la
perforación forma un confortable
reposacabezas.

POR
A cadeira Darwin usa uma estrutura
de balanço livre que inclui umas
duzentas lâminas de impressas anexas.
Quando a lâmina superior se suja,
o usuário simplesmente a arranca,
transformando assim a aparência
da cadeira. Quanto mais lâminas se
arrancam, a perfuração forma um
cômodo apoio de cabeça.

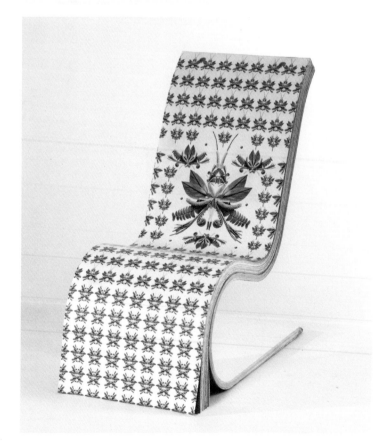

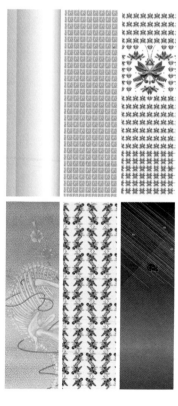

PLANTABLE

DESIGN FIRM
JAILmake

DESIGNERS
Liam Healy & Jamie Elliott

PHOTOGRAPHY
Zahra Shahabi

Plantable is hand made in the workshops of JAILmake in South East London, where each leg is hand bent and fillet brazed into the framework. A handmade, English-oak top is then placed over it, for plenty of space to sit around and enjoy passing the time. They are made to order in any color, size, or wood type.

FRA
Plantable est fabriquée à la main dans les ateliers de JAILmake, dans le sud-est de Londres. Le pliage des pieds et le brasage d'angle sur la structure sont réalisés manuellement. Le plateau en chêne anglais, façonné également à la main, est ensuite fixé. Sa grande taille fournit un espace convivial où les gens aiment se retrouver pour passer un bon moment. Les tables Plantable sont faites à la demande suivant les dimensions, la couleur et le type de bois choisis par le client.

ESP
Plantable se fabrica a mano en los talleres de JAILmake en el sureste de Londres, donde se dobla a mano las patas y se sueldan a la la estructura. A continuación se instala sobre ella una superficie de roble inglés hecha a mano para que los usuarios dispongan de un amplio espacio para sentarse y disfrutar del paso del tiempo. Se fabrican por encargo en todos los colores, tamaños y tipos de madera.

POR
Plantável é feito à mão nas oficinas de JAILmake no sudeste de Londres, onde cada perna se dobra à mão e se solda com malha dentro da estrutura. Então se coloca em cima uma superfície de carvalho inglês feita à mão, para que haja muito espaço para sentar-se em volta e desfrutar da passagem do tempo. São feitas conforme pedido em qualquer cor, tamanho ou tipo de madeira.

HOX — SOFT AND FOLDING FURNITURE

DESIGN FIRM
Asaf Yogev Design

DESIGNER
Asaf Yogev

PHOTOGRAPHY
Oded Antman & Liron Achdut

The HOX project stemmed primarily from the magical way in whichsponge changes shape when it is folded, and how it changes slightly with our body when we sit on it. The designer took the change that happens in the sponge to the extreme, so that the "byproduct" that our body creates in the sponge—that change, that indent— will create a different and surprising object when sitting on it.

FRA

Le projet HOX repose avant tout sur la capacité de l'éponge à changer de forme lorsqu'elle est pliée et à s'adapter au corps de la personne qui s'assoit dessus. Le designer a poussé cette propension jusqu'à l'extrême pour que l'empreinte laissée par la personne représente à chaque fois un objet différent et insolite.

ESP

El proyecto HOX surge básicamente de la manera mágica en la que la esponja cambia de forma cuando se dobla y se adapta sutilmente a nuestro cuerpo cuando nos sentamos sobre ella. El diseñador ha llevado al extremo la transformación que sufre la esponja, de manera que el efecto que nuestro cuerpo obra en ella, ese cambio, esa muesca, crea un objeto diferente y sorprendente cuando nos sentamos.

POR

O projeto HOX surgiu principalmente da maneira mágica com que a esponja muda de forma quando se dobra e como se altera levemente com nosso corpo, quando nos sentamos em cima. O designer tomou a alteração que sucede na esponja até o extremo, de forma que o derivado que nosso corpo cria na esponja ——essa alteração, essa marca— criará um objeto diferente e surpreendente quando nos sentemos em cima.

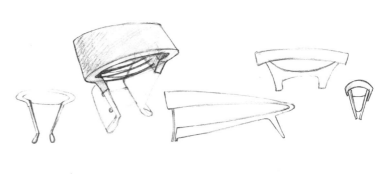

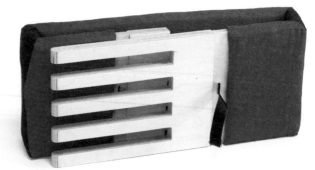

MONTANARA

DESIGN FIRM
Meritalia

DESIGNER
Gaetano Pesce

PHOTOGRAPHY
Meritalia Spa

The padding of Montanara is a polyurethane water lily, while the upholstery is digitally-printed, 100 percent cotton fabric. The structure is made from steel and wood. Designer Gaetano Pesce named it Montanara because he holds the belief that nature is a dear and wonderful companion that human beings have to treat with love.

FRA
Le rembourrage des meubles Montanara est un nénuphar en polyuréthane, et le tissu en 100 % coton est imprimé numériquement. La structure est en acier et bois. Le concepteur Gaetano Pesce a baptisé la collection Montanara parce qu'il considère que la nature est une précieuse et merveilleuse compagne que les êtres humains doivent aimer de tout leur cœur.

ESP
Montanara está relleno de poliuretano Waterlily y la tapicería es tela 100 % de algodón impresa digitalmente. La estructura es de acero y madera. El diseñador Gaetano Pesce le ha dado este nombre porque cree que la naturaleza es un compañero querido y maravilloso al que los seres humanos debemos tratar con amor.

POR
O recheio de Montanara é um poliuretano Waterlily, enquanto que o estofamento é de tecido 100 % de algodão impresso digitalmente. A estrutura é feita de aço e madeira. O designer Gaetano Pesce o denominou "Montanara" porque crê que a natureza é um companheiro querido e maravilhoso que os seres humanos devemos tratar com amor.

PICCOLA VIA LATTEA

DESIGN FIRM
Meritalia

DESIGNER
Mario Bellini

PHOTOGRAPHY
Meritalia Spa

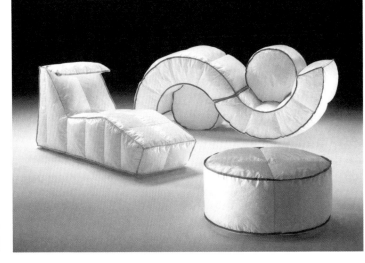

Not many people think that there should be armchairs, sofas, and chaise longues that are designed just for children. And simply reducing the scale of a piece of furniture does not usually yield satisfactory results. However, the Piccola Via Lattea series, designed to be made from simple, lightweight materials (translucent fabric made from recycled plastic and bubble wrap), is the proof that this reduction in scale can work. In fact, Piccola Via Lattea furniture actually looks like it was designed specifically for a little girl. Is such a thing possible? Well, yes, it is. Just look at Oliviero Toscani's incredible photography and you can see that now design is for children too. The internal padding is made of polyethylene and upholstered with polypropylene, both of which are recyclable materials.

FRA
Ce n'est pas tout le monde qui pense qu'il doit y avoir des fauteuils, des canapés et des chaises longues conçus spécialement pour les enfants. Lorsque l'on réduit simplement l'échelle d'un siège standard, on n'obtient pas forcément un bon résultat. La série Piccola Via Lattea, créée dans des matériaux simples et légers (un tissu translucide obtenu à partir de plastique et papier bulle recyclé), est la preuve qu'une plus petite échelle peut être une réussite. En fait, on a l'impression que la série Piccola Via Lattea a été conçue spécialement pour une petite fille. C'est possible ? Mais oui ! Il suffit de voir les incroyables photos d'Oliviero Toscani pour comprendre que le design s'adresse aussi aux enfants. Le rembourrage intérieur est en polyéthylène et est recouvert de polypropylène, ces matériaux étant tous les deux recyclables.

ESP
No son muchos los que opinan que deberían diseñarse sillones, sofás y cheslones exclusivamente para niños. Y reducir la escala de los muebles no suele dar buenos resultados. Sin embargo, la serie "Pequeña Vía Láctea", que se fabrica con materiales ligeros y sencillos (tela translúcida de plástico reciclado y plástico de burbujas, es la prueba de que esta disminución de tamaño puede funcionar. De hecho, se diría que los muebles de Pequeña Vía Láctea han sido diseñados para una niña. ¿Es posible? Sí, en efecto. Observe la increíble fotografía de Oliviero Toscani y comprenderá que ahora el diseño también es para niños. Los muebles están rellenos de polietileno y tapizados con polipropileno, ambos materiales reciclables.

PGR
Não muitas pessoas pensam que deveria haver poltronas, sofás e chaise longues desenhadas só para crianças. E reduzir simplesmente a escala do móvel normalmente não dá resultados satisfatórios. No entanto, a série Pequena Via Láctea, concebida para ser feita a partir de materiais leves e simples (tecido translúcido feito de plástico reciclado e plástico de bolhas), é a prova de que esta redução da escala pode funcionar. De fato, o mobiliário Pequena Via Láctea parece que foi desenhado em concreto para uma menina. É possível? Sim, é. Olhe a incrível fotografia de Oliviero Toscani e verá que agora o design também é para crianças. O recheio interno é feito de polietileno e estofado com polipropileno, ambos os materiais recicláveis.

THE IDEA OF A TREE

DESIGN FIRM
mischer'traxler

DESIGNERS
Katharina Mischer & Thomas Traxler

PHOTOGRAPHY
mischer'traxler

How does it all work, and what are the results? The machine Recorder One starts producing when the sun rises and stops when it sets. After sunset, the finished object can be "harvested." It slowly grows the object, by pulling threads through a coloring device and a glue basin and finally winding them around a mold. The length and/or height of the resulting object depend on the number of hours of daylight that particular day. The thickness of the layer and the color depend on the amount of solar energy, meaning that more sun equals a thicker layer and a paler color, while less sun equals a thinner layer and a darker color. This direct correlation between input and output makes changes in the object visual and readable.
The product becomes a three-dimensional representation of the day and the space where it was produced and communicates certain characteristics of locality, hinting at a new way of looking at this theme. This "industrialized locality" is not so much about local culture, craftsmanship, or resources. Instead, it deals with the climatic and environmental factors of the process's surroundings.

FRA

Mais comment cela fonctionne-t-il et quels résultats obtient-on avec ce procédé ? La machine enregistreuse lance la production au lever du soleil et l'arrête à son coucher, l'objet terminé étant « cueilli » à ce moment-là. Au cours du processus, l'objet prend forme lentement, à partir de fils tirés passant à travers un applicateur de couleurs et un bac de colle, qui s'enroulent ensuite autour d'un moule. La longueur et/ou la hauteur de l'objet résultant dépend du nombre d'heures d'ensoleillement ce jour-là. L'épaisseur et la couleur de la couche obtenue varient suivant la quantité d'énergie solaire. Plus de soleil signifie une plus grande épaisseur et une couleur plus pâle et, à l'inverse, moins de soleil produit une moindre épaisseur et un ton plus foncé. Ainsi, la correspondance entre l'énergie entrante et le résultat produit traduit les changements au cœur même de l'objet sous une forme visuelle et lisible. Le produit est une représentation en trois dimensions du jour et de l'espace où il a été produit et transmet certaines caractéristiques de son environnement local. C'est une nouvelle façon d'aborder le sujet du temps et de l'espace. Cette « régionalisation » de la production ne s'intéresse pas à la culture, ni à l'artisanat ou les ressources du coin. Elle s'attache uniquement aux facteurs climatiques et environnementaux en vigueur lors de la fabrication de l'objet.

ESP

¿Cómo funciona todo esto y cuáles son los resultados? El dispositivo Recorder One se pone en marcha cuando amanece y se detiene cuando anochece. Después se "cosecha" el objeto acabado, que crece poco a poco tirando de los hilos, que atraviesan un dispositivo de coloreado y un cuenco con cola, y enrollándolos en torno a un molde. El largo y/o el ancho del objeto resultante dependen del número de horas de sol de la jornada. El grosor de la capa y el color de la misma dependen de la cantidad de energía solar, siendo más gruesa y más clara si es mucha y más fina y oscura si es poca. Gracias a esta correlación directa entre la aportación y la producción, los cambios en los objetos son visibles y legibles. El producto se convierte de esta forma en una representación en tres dimensiones del día y el espacio en los que se ha creado y transmite ciertas características locales, sugiriendo una nueva perspectiva sobre este tema. Esta "localización industrializada" no refleja tanto la cultura, la artesanía o los recursos locales como los factores climáticos y medioambientales del proceso.

POR

Como funciona tudo isto, e quais os resultados? A máquina Recorder One começa a produzir quando sai o sol e para quando o sol se põe. Depois do anoitecer, pode-se "colher" o objeto acabado. Lentamente o objeto cresce, puxando fios através de um dispositivo de cor e uma tigela com cola e finalmente os enrola em volta de um molde. O comprimento e/ou largura do objeto resultante depende do número de horas de sol nesse dia em concreto. A espessura da camada e a cor dependem da quantidade de energia solar, o que significa que mais sol equivale a uma camada mais grossa e a uma cor mais pálida, enquanto menos sol equivale a uma camada mais fina e uma cor mais escura. Esta correlação direta entre a entrada e a saída faz com que as alterações no objeto sejam visuais e legíveis. O produto se converte numa representação tridimensional do dia e do espaço onde ocorreu e comunica certas características de localidade, apontando para uma nova forma de olhar a este assunto. Esta "localidade industrializada" não é tanto sobre cultura local, artesanato ou recursos. Em seu lugar, trata com os fatores climático e ambiental do ambiente do processo.

PARASITE FARM

DESIGNERS
Charlotte Dieckmann & Nils Ferber

PHOTOGRAPHY
Alexander Giesemann

How can urban humankind return to this natural basis of live? The poetic answer to that question is the Parasite Farm, a system that enables you to compost your biological waste, produce humus soil, and grow your own vegetables and herbs—all within your apartment! The cycle begins where food becomes waste: on the cutting board, which is also the cover of the vermicompost container. The cutting board can be slid aside to easily shove food scraps into the container. Inside the container there are microorganisms, tiger worms, and soil biota that break down the food scraps and make their nutrients available for plants. In this way, waste becomes valuable organic material again. The user is provided with homemade vermicompost. A built-in fly trap prevents the possibility of fruit flies escaping into your kitchen. The nutrient-rich humus provides the base for growing vegetables and herbs on your bookshelf. The user can harvest and savor his fresh nutriments and recycle the plant remains in the vermicompost container, which eventually completes the nutrient cycle.

ESP

¿Cómo podemos los seres urbanos recuperar nuestra forma de vida natural? La respuesta poética a esta pregunta es la granja de parásitos, un sistema mediante el que fabricamos abono con nuestros propios residuos biológicos, producimos mantillo y cultivamos verduras y hierbas en nuestro propio apartamento. El ciclo comienza donde la comida se convierte en residuo: en la tabla, que asimismo es la cubierta del contenedor de vermicompostado. La tabla puede apartarse para que arrojemos los restos de comida al contenedor. Dentro del mismo hay microorganismos, lombrices rojas y edafón que descomponen los restos de comida para que las plantas absorban sus nutrientes. De este modo la basura vuelve a convertirse en material orgánico valioso. El usuario obtiene vermicompostado casero. Un atrapamoscas incorporado impide que las moscas de la fruta se cuelen en la cocina. El mantillo rico en nutrientes es la base con la que se cultivan verduras y hierbas en las estanterías. El usuario puede cosechar los nutrientes frescos, disfrutarlos y reciclar los restos de la planta en el contenedor de vermicompostado, completando de este modo el ciclo de nutrientes.

FRA

Comment la population urbaine peut-elle assurer son retour à la nature ? La réponse poétique à cette question est le système Parasite Farm, qui permet de transformer en compost les déchets organiques, de produire de l'humus et de faire pousser des légumes et des herbes aromatiques dans son propre appartement. Le cycle commence là où une partie des aliments se transforme en déchets, à savoir, au niveau de la planche à découper qui tient lieu de couvercle à la vermicompostière. On peut faire glisser la planche pour déverser facilement les déchets dans le bac. À l'intérieur de celui-ci, il y a des microorganismes, des vers de fumier et des composantes biotiques qui vont décomposer les déchets alimentaires et récupérer leurs nutriments qui serviront à nourrir les plantes. Les déchets deviennent alors un précieux matériau organique. Le système fournit à l'utilisateur un vermicompost fait maison. Une trappe anti-moucherons empêche ces insectes de s'échapper et d'envahir votre cuisine. L'humus, riche en nutriments, fournit l'élément de base qui va vous permettre de faire pousser des légumes et des herbes aromatiques sur vos étagères. Vous pourrez ensuite cueillir et savourer votre récolte et recycler les restes des plantes dans le bac à vermicompost, bouclant ainsi le cycle nutritif.

POR

Como pode a humanidade urbana voltar à sua base natural de vida? A resposta poética a esta pergunta é a Granja de parasitas, um sistema que lhe permite adubar a partir de seus próprios desperdícios biológicos, produzir húmus e cultivar seus próprios vegetais e ervas, e tudo dentro de seu apartamento. O ciclo começa onde a comida se converte em desperdício: na tábua de cortar, que também é a cobertura para o contêiner da lumbricultura. A tabela de cortar desliza para um lado para lançar os restos de comida ao contêiner. Dentro do contêiner há microorganismos, minhocas vermelhas, e edafon que decompõem os restos de comida e transformam seus nutrientes em nutrientes disponíveis para as plantas. Deste modo, o lixo se torna outra vez material orgânico valioso. O usuário obtém lumbricultura caseira. Uma armadilha inserida para moscas evita a possibilidade de as moscas de fruta escapem por sua cozinha. O húmus rico em nutrientes proporciona a base para cultivar vegetais e ervas em sua estante. O usuário pode colher e saborear seus nutrientes frescos e reciclar os restos de planta no contêiner da lumbricultura, o que, ao final, completa o ciclo de nutrientes.

A / Z